To my mother:
In gratitude for all the devotion she had for God's work and her
family. "Let her own works praise her in the gates."

THE CROWNING CHARACTER OF THE VIRTUOUS WOMAN

Proverbs 31:10

Can you believe we have already entered the first week of January, a new month, and a new year! I find it quite motivating to have the old year behind me and the New Year ahead of me... It's kind of like a clean slate; a chance to start over, to start fresh. If you pay attention to the catalogs you receive in the mail, you would perceive that one of the things people typically work on in the month of January are inside home improvements. With the weather getting colder outside, it is natural to withdraw inside where it is warm and there keep ourselves busy. As we turn our focus toward the inside of our homes, we begin to notice the flaws that reside there. A fresh coat of paint might need applying; drapes need laundering or even changing; old color schemes have to go; a set of table and chairs might need refinishing or replacing; the purchasing and hanging of wallpaper could bring just the right atmosphere; overstuffed closets need cleaning and reorganizing etc. Many people even take this time to completely remodel certain rooms during the first few months of the year and a variety of necessary items are placed on sale in stores and catalogs for just this reason. Perhaps you have already taken an inward look at your home and considered doing some of these things yourself. Maybe you've even taken an inward look at your heart and considered some things that need to be remodeled or refreshed as well... I hope so!

Over the course of the passing year, there are many areas in a woman's life that are neglected and there comes a time when we need to devote our attentions to the things that are lacking, amen? That is why I have decided to resend the series on the Proverbs 31 woman every New Year. It is a good time for all of us to refresh and remodel our hearts and minds using the Word of God and the godly example of this woman in scripture. Those who desire to be truly beloved, respected, useful, and honorable should study this description **daily**! As always, there are new subscribers to Rise and Shine who have not received this study, and I would like to give them the opportunity to do so now. Together we can all purpose in our hearts to be vessels meet for the Master's use this New Year, and prepared unto every good work, amen? I want to be a blessing to others, as I am confident each of you does as well. I want to begin in my home and be a blessing to each member there. I want to begin with my husband....

Proverbs 31:10, "Who can find a virtuous woman? for her price is far above rubies."

Why does a virtuous woman have to be so hard to find?? Can she not be the norm instead of an almost extinct type of woman? Has your husband been fortunate enough to find such a woman in you, dear lady? What does the word virtuous mean? In Webster's 1828 Dictionary, it is defined as: morally good, practicing moral duties, abstaining from vice. In the Word of God in Proverbs 12:4 we find this definition: "A virtuous woman is a **crown** to her husband...."

If asked, would your husband be able to say you are a crown to him? What exactly do you think it means to be a **crown** to your husband? (Not a crown of thorns either!) As I further studied it's meaning, I found this to be a very interesting concept when applied to the role we have as wives....

<u>A crown:</u>

is a badge of imperial or regal power
shows dignity
bestows honor
exemplifies kingly government/authority
is an adornment
brings completion

What an application we can gain from this definition! First, I want each of you to close your eyes and imagine a crown sitting all by itself on a chair next to a king. Now imagine that king sitting all by himself without a crown. Each of these thoughts present to us an incomplete picture… Now I want you to place the crown on the king's head and discover what a transformation takes place, what magnificence suddenly surrounds him! What strength of presence the king now carries with him when entering a room - and all because of a crown…You see ladies, the crown is his completion, reminding others of the king's authority, his power, his dignity, his honor. It is an adornment to his person. Oh, how we need to be that to our husbands today! We ought to add to their character as a crown does to the king… Yes, as wives, we ought to make it easy for our husbands to say that they have found a rarity; they have found a virtuous woman, amen? Are you surrounding your husband with magnificence, dear wife? If not, perhaps it is time to refresh and remodel… No wonder the Bible says her price is far above rubies, for such a woman truly IS hard to find! Can you yourself think of a woman today in your sphere of influence that you would consider a crown to her husband? No doubt, you will have to do some searching, for most women today - **Christian** women - are subtracting from the dignity, honor, power, and authority of their husbands.

Many married men or "kings" are walking around without a crown, they are incomplete.... Many women today are competing with their husbands rather than completing them! They are competing for attention, authority, power, and honor. These women are easy to find - just look in the driver seats of most cars - and you will find that the women are leading the men around! Ladies, a crown does not fight for attention but rather is content to rest upon the king's head and compliment his position. I know this is not a popular message with the women of the world today - and even with many Christian women - but guess what? It's Bible, and it is **right**!

Let's go on to think about where the crown is placed for a moment... It is set upon the king's head. It fits him perfectly. It is not so small that it goes unnoticed or becomes lost in his kingly hairdo! It is just right for him. Nor is it so big that it falls down in his face and blocks his vision, thereby causing him to trip and fall. Again, it is a perfect fit and one so perfect that no matter which way the king leans the crown remains intact.

Ladies, can we say such is our conduct when our husbands lean in a direction that we do not agree with? Or is that one of the times we, as crowns, decide to slip off the king's head completely?? You see, a perfectly fit crown will gracefully retain it's position of adornment, reminding others of the power, dignity, honor, and authority of the king at all times. Imagine a king giving a solemn decree as he leads others, and the crown sliding off his head at that precise moment, subtracting from his authority and mocking his character. As his wife, a woman of crowning character respects the heart and mind of her king and sits closely by, enhancing his every decision! Yes ,ladies, a virtuous woman is a **crown** to her husband, and the Bible goes on to say in that very same verse; "but she that maketh ashamed is as rottenness in his bones." Which role are you fulfilling in your husband's life today??

Ruth 3:11 says, "...for all the city of my people doth know that thou art a virtuous woman."

Can this be said of us today, Christian women? Is this your personal testimony? Whenever your name is mentioned, do people KNOW you as a virtuous woman? If not, it is a great goal to have this year, amen? Why does being a **virtuous** woman have to be something that is a rarity? Why can't it be the character trait of many women rather than just a small handful? We who know the Lord have the potential to be truly virtuous women! Because of the indwelling presence of the Holy Spirit, godly traits can dwell within us; they can abound as we continually yield to the Spirit's control and exhibit the crowning character of Jesus Christ. Ladies, the Bible says there is great value to godly inner beauty.... Let us refresh and remodel, let us do whatever is necessary in our hearts to carry this beauty forward with us into this New Year! Let this be the desire of all our hearts - to keep the virtuous woman alive, and to prevent her from "slipping" away, or from becoming extinct altogether.

In closing, when a man has found a virtuous woman, the Bible says he has found wisdom (Pr. 3:13-18). He has found a crown for himself! No precious jewels or earthly treasures are worthy to be compared with true wisdom, which is why the value of a virtuous woman is far above the value of rubies. Her wisdom is found in God's Word, the crowning of her character! Ladies, that is why **every** day this year we must make God's wisdom our supreme business. Are you willing to part with all for it? This wisdom is the Lord Jesus Christ and His salvation, sought and obtained by faith and prayer. Seek after God's wisdom this year, and you will have increased your value as a woman immensely!

THE HEART OF THE VIRTUOUS WOMAN

Proverbs 31:11

I hope you are all looking forward to our continued study of the ever- haunting Proverbs 31 woman. I wonder why we all feel that way about her. Is it that difficult to live out the example that God has given us in this portion of scripture? Or on the other hand, could it be that we just might not be willing to go that far ourselves.... Ladies, I hope that we will prayerfully and open-mindedly allow the Lord to convince and convict us each in the areas we each need to grow in as we spend time getting to know her more intimately. It is a matter of the heart, is it not? The heart of the virtuous woman is what we need to get a picture of and implant in our own bosom. Why? The heart is the inner part of her, the chief part, the vital part. It is the center of spiritual activity. It is the home of her personal life. It is where life is preserved and where all operations of even human life are centered. It is the seat of our conscience where it's affections, passions, love, joy, guilt, courage, motives, pleasure etc. exist. Getting to know the heart of the virtuous woman will make her example an easy one to follow and remove it's haunting affect upon us as we adopt her godly perspective as our own. Let's get started as we study verse 11 which says:

"The heart of her husband doth safely trust in her, so that he shall have no need of spoil." If the heart of the virtuous woman is key, and the hub of all spiritual and physical life, then such is the case with her husband as well! The heart is also <u>his</u> chief part. It is also <u>his</u> vital part. It is the seat of <u>his</u> conscience. It is the home of <u>his</u> personal life.

Moreover, scripture says that his heart safely trusts in his wife's heart - if she is a virtuous woman. Yes, the core of his being trusts in the core of her being.... What an honor to be so trustworthy! The question is though, how important is your husband's heart to YOU, dear wife?? Does his heart safely TRUST in your heart today? Do you even care??

Of course, I looked up the definition of **trust** so we could get the full impact of the word through it's meaning. Trust is defined as: comfort, strengthen, place confidence in, resting of the mind on the integrity, veracity (habitual observance of truth), justice, friendship or other sound principle of another person - present or future.

Ladies, when your husband's heart is able to safely trust in you in the manner described above, he is completely free from all worry. Even from the very threat of it, he is free! He is confident in your integrity, your veracity, your fairness, and your friendship in the present. Your husband rests in your future loyalty as well as in the present; there is no threat of you ever leaving him. What a deep-rooted foundation this provides for marital communication and love! What harmony takes place in the home when such trust is present, directly stemming from the condition of the heart of the virtuous woman.

Proverbs 4:23, "Keep thy heart with all diligence; for out of it are the issues of life."

Ladies, how is it possible for the condition of our hearts to be so healthy, so effectual, so instrumental in the life of our husbands? The answer is very simple.... We find in scripture that the virtuous woman makes the Lord her trust, thereby allowing her to be someone who can be trusted in! Turn with me to 1 Peter 3 and let's look at verses 1-5....

"Likewise, ye wives, be in subjection to your own husbands..."

Now I know most women stop right here after this point in the verse and say, "That's not for me!" But ladies, if your heart is fully trusting in the Lord, then your husband's heart can fully trust in you to be in subjection to him, amen?

Let me give you an example. One year, as my husband and I were packing his things for his missions trip to Mexico, I asked him if he would mind if I drove 10 hours to Florida to visit my parents while he was gone. Naturally, his response was one of concern for my safety without a man in the car to protect and guide me; therefore, his answer was a firm, "no way!" I did not argue as I had a feeling what his answer would be. But ladies, after listening to his heartfelt concerns, I saw that my husband's heart would not have been at peace while away on the missions trip for concern over my safety, and I did not want to be responsible for placing worry there and distracting him from his other responsibilities. Through trusting the Lord, my heart was willing to put my actions in subjection to my husband's wishes because his heart is important to me! Now some would think that not fair and would say that I should be able to have the ability to decide such a thing for myself and not have to be accountable to him. I know the world would surely laugh at me for submitting. But it is important to me that my husband is able to rest in me and have no need of spoil, as the Bible says should be the case. I trust the leadership of the Lord in my husband's life and I trust that the Lord will not only protect, but also bless me for being in subjection to my husband's wishes. Bucking and arguing with him would do nothing more than damage our marital relationship and subtract from his heart's ability to safely trust in me. It should be the same in all areas of our life together, not just in traveling decisions, amen?

There are far too many women living and making decisions as if they were not married at all! Ladies, we should be willing to yield to our husband's authority and leadership and make ourselves accountable to them, for in so doing we are causing their trust in us to grow and bringing protection and blessing upon ourselves and our marriages, proving our trust in the Lord.

Proverbs 3:5&6, "Trust in the Lord with all thine heart; and lean not unto thine own understanding. In all thy ways acknowledge him, and he shall direct thy paths."

Yes, our trust in God is our strength to submit both willingly and lovingly as verse 5 of 1 Peter points out, "For after this manner in the old time the holy women also, who trusted in God, adorned themselves, being in subjection to their own husbands." You see ladies, the secret of the virtuous woman's heart being a safe place for her husband is the Lord first being her safe place of trust! Trusting in God brings forth the fruit of being in subjection to her husband. It is part of her adornment, what she wears every day. Submission is what makes up part of a virtuous woman's beauty. It is in the sight of God of great price, a value soon realized by her husband. Likewise, the lack thereof is not unnoticed by the man whose wife is bankrupt of such godly character! Perhaps you have struggled with this area of being in subjection to your husband... You had better take a long look at your trust in God - it probably needs some remodeling and refreshing this year!

Let's continue on by taking a look at the last half of Proverbs 31:11 which says; "...so that he shall have no need of spoil."

By this, we see that a virtuous woman makes it her business to see to her husband's good. She can be trusted to the faithful management of things. Spoil is defined as: to corrupt, to cause to decay and perish, to ruin, to mar, to render useless by injury, to destroy, to injure fatally, to pull asunder, to lose valuable qualities. Are you guilty of bringing any of these conditions upon your husband or your home? Do you have a destructive nature or a constructive one....

Proverbs 14:1, "Every wise woman buildeth her house: but the foolish plucketh it down with her hands."

Ladies, if we are going to strive to be virtuous women, we need to take concern for the protection of our marriages and our husbands. We should never want to see spoil come upon them. We should not want to bring any damaging circumstances into our husband's lives by misconduct of our own behavior, whether in word or deed. We should uphold the value of our marriages and see to it that we are adding to the value of our relationships every day by make large contributions to them. We should also be faithful in many other areas as well, such as the spending of money, the way we speak about our husbands, careful about the places we go, select in the activities we become involved in etc. True, husbands should be equally concerned over such matters, but we are looking at **our** hearts today, so do not let the enemy distract your focus and place it on your husband by thinking, "Well, what about him?!" We are going to trust God with our men, just like the holy women of old time did, remember?
 While we have been looking at things COMMITTED that can bring unrest to our husband's hearts, let us stop for a moment and look at the things OMITTED that can cause an unrest and inability of them to safely trust in us. Search your heart, dear lady.... What things can you think of right now that you have left undone that are displeasing to your husband?

The laundry? The house-cleaning? Is there disorganization everywhere you look? What requests has he made of you recently that you have placed at the bottom of your list of priorities - sewing a button on, making a phone call, running an errand, paying a particular bill etc. Maybe he would like to open the cupboard just once and find a snack HE loves....
Ladies, these small little incidences add up and become the very things that subtract from our husband's hearts safely trusting in us. Little things can be the cause for spoil or decay taking place in our marriages. Protect your home from spoil; don't be the cause of it, amen?

Maybe you are one who has the whole house in order and there is not a speck of dust found anywhere. What about the attention and love your husband has needed? Have we been neglecting our husbands in this area, ladies? We can have the cleanest houses and the coldest hearts and what kind of a home is that to come to at the end of the day! Has your husband's heart been able to safely trust in you for warmth and physical affection, praise and honor? It is one of the special privileges of marriage to come together in physical unity - yet why do we cause our husbands to have to *earn* our love? Why is it not a natural result of our HEART attitude towards them? A heart that is trusting in God...

This is a serious topic, ladies and I want you to pay attention now. Look with me at Proverbs 5:19:

"Let her be as the loving hind and pleasant roe; let her breasts satisfy thee **at all times**; and be thou ravished **always** with her love."

"Let her be..." Inventory time! Are you being **loving,** dear lady?? Would your husband be able to say there is pleasantness to your love, or usually reluctance? Do you act as if it is a chore to love him or are you thankful for the privilege and opportunity to meet his physical needs? Ladies, do not be so foolish as to drive your man away from home - draw him into the warmth and love God has created to exist between husband and wife. It is for your husbands' good, so that he should have no need of spoil, and for the pleasure of you both! Ladies, the Bible clearly shows here that we are to be *actively* involved in the pursuit of loving our husbands. Why not chase HIM around for a change, instead of him always chasing you! God says to us here in this portion of scripture, wives, that our husbands are to be satisfied AND ravished.

Yes, I am going to look those two words up, so brace yourself! The word satisfied simply means to be made content. Do you have a husband who is content with your love, or is he suffering for lack of it? Wait until you hear what <u>ravished</u> means... It is defined as snatched away, delighted to ecstasy, to seize and carry away, transporting with delight, and compelling to submit. Now, if we apply that definition to scripture today, this means we are to snatch away our husbands and delight them to ecstasy! Need I say more?? Most of the time they are trying to snatch us away, trying to seize us and carry us off for a little romance and what do we do? Kick, scream, and try to escape, amen? This reluctance has to stop... We do have to become better at loving our husbands! How often are we to behave lovingly toward them? If you read Proverbs 5:19 again, you will notice the Bible says AT ALL TIMES and ALWAYS. There is no need for the Greek to understand that, amen? Are any of you falling short of what the Lord expects of you as a wife?

Still not convinced? Turn with me to Proverbs 7, read the whole chapter, and observe the downhill progression of a man that falls into the trap of a strange woman. Look at verse 25 & 26 for a moment, which say:

"Let not thine heart decline to her ways, go not astray in her paths. For she hath cast down many wounded: yea, many strong men have been slain by her."

I daresay that strong husbands whose hearts have not been able to safely trust in their wives for physical affection and warmth and satisfaction have suffered spoil as a result have ended up in the arms of a strange woman whose house is the way of death. It will be the death of your marriage also! Why contribute to the temptations a man faces daily in this area by withholding affection from your husband and causing him spoil? Remember, a virtuous woman's heart is a safe place for her husband and he shall have no need of decaying in his love for her. He has no need of injury by her, emotionally, physically, financially, or spiritually. He has no need of ruin by her. He will gain confidence in her, in her love and concern for him and his needs. He will not be an insecure man. He will gain confidence in the Lord she has made the trust of her heart. May this the testimony of our marriages – especially those of God's people! If it is not, may it be our goal to be such. If you are guilty of neglecting your husband's heart, why not go to him today and ask his forgiveness for not being the right kind of wife. Then ask God to give you the strength to grow as you learn to make the Lord your heart's trust. There is no spoil in the home of a virtuous woman!

THE DEVOTION OF THE VIRTUOUS WOMAN

Proverbs 31:12

I hope you are enjoying our time with the Proverbs 31 woman as much as I am! I need this reminder regularly, for it is easy to get off track and forget the things that are important as the days, the months, and even the whole year busily unfolds before me and time and opportunity to do right slips away.

We have seen the importance of being a crown to our husbands. We have seen the importance of our husband's heart being able to safely find trust in our hearts and the direction they are taking. Today we are going to look at the fruit of the Proverbs 31 woman's heart, the outward manifestation of her inward attitude. We learned that the heart is the center of all spiritual and physical activity. Let us therefore focus on the actions that are born of such a heart and determine the specific areas where each of us can improve…

Proverbs 31:12, "She will do him good and not evil all the days of her life."
The quality I see present here as described by this verse is loyalty. The virtuous woman is loyal to her husband. She has purposed to be so in her heart, and she carries that purpose out in her life. A loyal woman has a habit of being true and faithful not only to her God, but to her husband as well. Every great person has first learned **how** to obey, **whom** to obey, and **when** to obey, amen?

Given that thought, how do you demonstrate your loyalty, dear lady? Loyalty is demonstrated through an unwavering completion of responsibilities - no matter what the difficulties may be! A loyal woman will defend with determination her privilege to be obedient and faithful to the object of her loyalty. Which prompts me to ask you this question: WHO is the object of your loyalty today? Could it be that YOU are the object of your loyalty?? To be self-willed is to be disloyal to God AND to your husband! Nothing can cause the virtuous woman to be otherwise minded, for she has learned to die to self. She has purposed in her heart to remain loyal all the days of her life. Have you done as much? For the Proverbs 31 woman, loyalty is not a quality that is dependent upon *the actions of her husband*, but is rather a result of the condition of her heart and her relationship with the Lord. So often, we see and hear of marriages falling apart, even Christian marriages, as women selfishly decide that their husbands are not worthy of their loyalty for the most absurd reasons. Over the course of time, their eyes have been opened to their husband's imperfections and they simply decide that they will move out and move on. Husbands are viewed as nothing more than an object to be returned for a refund, much like we do when taking merchandise back to Wal-mart that has not performed satisfactorily or is found faulty. God help us if that is the depth of our marital loyalty! Have you found yourself wanting to throw in the towel because of recent or ongoing struggles in your marriage? You need to develop some loyalty, dear lady! Just the other day I heard of a young woman who, upon finding out that her husband is not able to produce children, has decided she no longer loves him and will move on. I wonder what she would have done if she had been diagnosed with cancer and he decided to walk out on her?? I daresay someone needs to speak to this woman of her need for loyalty, amen?

In addition, ladies, I hope when you observe such misconduct in women's lives within your sphere of influence, you will obey what God says to do in this portion of scripture below:

Titus 3:1-2, "Put them in mind to be subject to principalities and powers, to obey magistrates, to be ready to every good work, to speak evil of no man, to be no brawlers, but gentle, shewing all meekness unto all men."

For instance, there is a woman in my past who had asked that I stand up for her at her wedding. I don't know about you, but I take the responsibility of witnessing wedding vows seriously. Why? Because God does! Just two short years later this Christian woman decided that she no longer "clicked" with this man she married and filed for divorce. Prayerfully, I wrote her a nice long, tasteful letter putting her in remembrance of the vows I witnessed her make before God, and to her husband. She no longer speaks to me... Am I sorry for what I said because of the outcome? Absolutely not! I do not believe that if God expects us to be loyal to our husbands he would approve of us witnessing disloyalty to the institution of marriage with closed eyes and mouths. A virtuous woman will uphold that which she lives by - that which God upholds! Speak up for what is right ladies, and in the right manner. Disloyalty is defined as not true to allegiance, faithless, false in love, not constant, not true to the marriage bed. To summarize this point, may we groan within ourselves over a desire to be truly loyal to our husbands and encourage others to be so as well!

1 Corinthians 7:10 says, "And unto the married I command, yet not I, but the Lord, Let not the wife depart from her husband."

Before we ever leave our husbands in a physical sense, there will first be a departing from him within your heart. How is your **heart** doing towards your husband today? Has it remained loyal through thick and thin, stayed strong while going over those bumps in the road, or has your loyalty waned and even departed altogether? Perhaps you have experienced a lack of concern on your husband's part for you, for your marriage in general. What happens to your loyalty then? Does it waver, or does it remain in tact and make a difference in his life for good, and in the success of your marriage?

Ecclesiastes 10:4, "If the spirit of the ruler rise up against thee, leave not thy place; for yielding pacifieth great offences."

Ladies, if you yield to your pride or seeking revenge in an offensive marital circumstance, there is the danger of becoming disloyal to your husband! Are you hasty within your heart to quit your post in that moment of passion when offences come? It will only be a matter of time before the outward manifestation of that inward disloyalty will shine forth.... Take care dear lady, that your heart remains loyal to your husband, even in moments of trial, and lead others on to victory by your godly example! This may sound abrupt, but often loyalty consists in keeping your mouth shut! You see, your words will give your heart away.. Perhaps you have been in the company of other women, either at a social gathering, or in the work place, or maybe even at church, where Christian ladies are verbally disloyal to their husbands by talking them down and discoloring their reputations. Ladies, with disloyalty on our lips, we cause marriage to appear to be a curse rather than one of life's greatest blessings! Christian wife, I hope that you have not been guilty of being numbered with the transgressors.... Why not be different; strive to be a virtuous woman - the one that shows true loyalty to her husband and to the sacredness of marriage.

Guard your heart diligently against disloyalty!
Could there be the possibility of another woman being more loyal to your husband than you are??? Think about that for a moment as I place some emphasis on the different words in our verse today.

"**SHE** will do him good and not evil all the days of her life."

It is you who must be the one who is most loyal to your husband! Not the secretary at work, not your mother-in-law, not a neighbor, not the ladies in church, but YOU!

Let's look at it this way:

"She **WILL** do him good and not evil all the days of her life."

When we read it this way, we can see that PURPOSE is necessary. Have you purposed that you will remain loyal to your husband? Believe me, a woman that wants to steal away your husband will exhibit such determination! Better for you to be the one, amen?

Let's try this one:

"She will **DO** him good and not evil all the days of her life."

Ladies, loyalty shouldn't just sound like a good idea or just exist as nice thought in the back of your mind to one day apply to your life - get busy and make it happen now! Decide to put forth some effort in this matter! (Jn.13:17)

Here's a good one:

"She will do **HIM** good and not evil all the days of her life."

So often women are quick to serve other men and willingly tend to their needs while throwing a glare of disgust at their husbands for what is considered to be laziness if they ask for anything! Ever done that? Perhaps the pastor, or boss at work, or another man in church, maybe even another male family member will call with a request for your help and your response is, "Oh I'd love to do that for you - just ask me anytime, no problem at all!" Then we get home and it's, "Why can't you do it yourself?!" Your husband should be your priority and the one who FIRST deserves your loyalty. Don't give to another man what should belong to him!!

We're on a roll now, let's keep going with this one:

"She will do him **GOOD** and not evil all the days of her life."

All you have to do is sit down, make a list of what your husband considers good, as God would have it, and then see to it that you do it! What could be easier? :-) Be careful of those motives... We like to do good sometimes for certain purposes, don't we? Let's be sure it's a result of our loyalty and not because we have an ulterior motive to getting our own way!

Uh -oh, look at this one:

"She will do him good **AND NOT EVIL** all the days of her life." You mean, you can't serve him breakfast in bed with a bitter heart?! You mean, as long as the house is clean you can't be giving him the silent treatment for something else?! You mean, as long as you're nice to him in public and serve him around others so that you can "appear" to be a loyal wife, you can't expect him to get it himself at home?! You mean, if he starts the argument you can't use that as a license to call him a jerk?! Oh, why did the Bible have to go and say the, "<u>and not evil</u>" part - now we have to crucify our flesh!!

Yes, a virtuous woman adds AND subtracts, ladies! She adds the good and subtracts the evil. How has your marital math been coming out these days? I hope it makes up the sum of what is pleasing to the Lord!

We'll finish up with this one, the grand finale!

"She will do him good and not evil **ALL THE DAYS OF HER LIFE**."

There are no legitimate reasons why the virtuous woman stops doing right by her husband and starts doing wrong. No, she doesn't take time off during her menstrual cycle and treat him miserably one week of the month! The virtuous woman is always faithful and loyal to her husband regardless of his mistakes, his imperfections, his treatment of her, *and her feelings*. She uses her life wisely for a purpose, and that purpose is found in pleasing her husband and the Lord! We will look over in this study concerning the life of the Proverbs 31 woman many verses. But take note today that her list of admirable qualities begins with these particular verses of devotion to her husband. His needs are at the top of her list of priorities and she doesn't give him leftovers of her time and energy - he gets it FIRST! Before work, the kids, and yes, even the church....

A virtuous woman is a **loyal** woman. Would that be you?

THE ENDEAVORS OF THE VIRTUOUS WOMAN

Proverbs 31:13

Today the verse that we are going to focus on in our study of the Proverbs 31 woman is verse 13, which says of her, "She seeketh wool, and flax, and worketh willingly with her hands".

Let's begin by looking at the first part of that verse – "**She seeketh wool and flax**...."

The virtuous woman endeavors to find wool and flax because they are necessary items for producing clothing. In biblical times, flax was used to make linen, a common household chore, and quite a time consuming process! Women used wool to make clothing, blankets, and other articles. It was also a symbol of whiteness and purity....

Hosea 2:9 says, "...and will recover my wool and my flax given to cover her nakedness."

Purity of heart naturally gives birth to a sincere desire for properly covering oneself, and this matter of important business was next up on the virtuous woman's list of priorities! She endeavored to modestly cover herself, knowing how important it is to the Lord that our nakedness not be displayed. The virtuous woman sought after the material necessary to accomplish this priority in her life, such as the wool and flax God provided.

How about us, ladies? Is it as important to us that our nakedness be covered? Have you stopped to consider whether you are modestly dressed as far as the Lord is concerned? Sad to say, but even in the church today there are many women who are provocatively dressed and it ought not so to be! The virtuous woman **seeks** to cover herself and be modest in her appearance. That means she goes to "great lengths" to see that this mission is accomplished. She is not a victim of fashion choices in the stores, or limited by the lack of modest choices available. She simply takes matters into her own hands and becomes responsible for finding a way to clothe herself adequately. Her choice of fabric is not one of tightness nor sheerness, but that which is conservative and in keeping with a godly nature.

Proverbs 7:10, "And, behold, there met him a woman with the attire of an harlot, and subtil of heart."
The reflection of any woman's heart is revealed in her choice of attire as shown by this verse above. Notice the contrast as we consider the harlot and how her heart is known through her choice of clothing. She is professing her very nature…
Now go open your closet door and look inside. What does your clothing reveal about YOUR heart, dear lady?? Does it send out the message that you are subtil of heart? Subtil is defined as sly, cunning, crafty, and insinuating. What are you *insinuating* with your clothing? Are you advertising something you ought not to? Perhaps you need to take a longer look in the mirror and prayerfully consider the choices you have been making in your wardrobe selections! Yes, the virtuous woman willingly - not the least bit reluctantly – endeavors to find clothing that would reflect purity of heart - the heart that her husband safely trusts in! Can your husband's heart rest in your clothing choices, dear lady, or does it cause him concern due to the improper attention it may bring you from the opposite sex?

What motive is dictating your clothing purchases today - a desire to be 'in fashion', or a desire to reflect godliness? May God help us to view our clothing through HIS holy eyes and not the world's eyes, amen?

Can your husband's heart rest in your clothing choices, dear lady, or does it cause him concern due to the improper attention it may bring you from the opposite sex? What motive is dictating your clothing purchases today - a desire to be 'in fashion', or a desire to reflect godliness? May God help us to view our clothing through HIS holy eyes and not the world's eyes, amen?

1 Timothy 2:9&10 says, "In like manner also, that women adorn themselves in modest apparel with shamefacedness and sobriety; not with broided hair, or gold, or pearls, or costly array; but (which becometh women professing godliness) with good works."

Perhaps you mistakenly think that you will not be attractive apart from wearing seductive, gaudy, or highly expensive clothing. The Bible says in the above verse that the adornment of good works is the most beautiful attire we could ever be dressed in! Our character should shine forth more than anything else, not our bodylines. As Christian women, we ought to be diligent about decorating our hearts with godly character traits, for they are the gold and pearls and costly array that the Lord would prefer to see adorning His daughters! Hence, if the Lord truly has control of your heart, He will have control of your closet too! Unfortunately, many Christian women have forsaken their inward beauty in sole pursuit of the outward…. We rarely look for wool and flax anymore as the virtuous woman did. It's time we 're-covered' ourselves from the world, amen?

Now we'll look at the second part of Proverbs 31:13 which says, "....**and worketh willingly with her hands.**"

Knowing that the wool and flax had to be prepared for use as clothing, one can understand that the virtuous woman was a worker. She was not able to indulge in a life of ease. I'm sure there were many other duties required of her position in the home that we will look at in the days ahead. However, one thing was certain, laziness was not a part of her character! She worked, and she worked willingly!

Ladies, you may not realize it, but this attitude contributes to our inward beauty, just as a poor attitude subtracts from it.... The virtuous woman did not feel sorry for herself in her duties as she carried them out, but rather her heart was joyful in every task she accomplished. You have to admit, we do not have it nearly as hard as this woman did, yet the Bible says she was able to still work willingly, therefore we ought to be REALLY happy seeing we have so many technological luxuries in our day. You and I can walk into the kitchen and push a button for coffee, push a button for dinner in the microwave, push a button for the dishes to be cleaned, turn a knob to start the wash, and turn a knob to start the dryer! Then why is it there are more women on anti-depressants and miserable about being at home than ever before?? Perhaps hard work is **good** for us, amen?! It's health to our hearts and minds.... Let's be known as workers, ladies! More than that, let's be known as WILLING workers! What is your heart attitude toward your work at home today? Have you been walking past that pile of laundry and sticking your tongue out at it? Are you serving dinner with slumped shoulders and a chin hanging down to the floor? Do you find yourself lying in bed longer and longer each day, not willing to face the responsibilities that have fallen on your shoulders in the running of your household? Do you do great one week and then lousy the next because of your roller-coaster attitude?

Does your family view you as a woman who is content in your role within the home? Do you *care* what attitudes they see in you as you go about your work? God does.... Remember moms, your daughters will pack up and carry off with them into their home the very same perspective you had toward your work at home! A sobering thought, indeed! May the grace of God put gladness into our hearts, and a lustre upon our countenances, amen? The Lord must establish the work of a virtuous woman's hands. Instead of wasting our precious, fleeting days in whining, complaining, feeling sorry for ourselves, pursuing various fancies, or just being lazy, let us strive to be sure that the beauty of holiness may always be seen in our conduct....

Psalm 90:17, "And let the beauty of the Lord our God be upon us: and establish thou the work of our hands upon us; yea, the work of our hands establish thou it."

Consider your hands for a moment. Do your realize that our hands are our most valuable instruments? A virtuous woman accomplishes much good through her hands, as we will continue to discover. Proverbs 14:1 says, "Every wise woman buildeth her house, but the foolish plucketh it down with her hands." Are you constructing your home with a willingness to work or is your laziness plucking it down bit by bit? If so, ask God to renew your heart attitude. So many homes today are nothing more than a pit-stop for family members. From the outside looking in, things appear as if they are running smoothly, yet within those very same homes disorganization, discontent, and disarray are dwelling as prominent members! A virtuous woman does not allow such conditions to take place in her home. She protects herself and her family from such a poverty stricken lifestyle, and provides the example of a *willing worker*. Like Christ, the virtuous woman understands that her work is **God's** work for her. She intends to glorify Him in it, and rests in the fact that the rewards are eternal....

John 17:4, "I have glorified thee on the earth: I have finished the work which thou gavest me to do."

In closing, I want to leave you with this man's testimony of his wife and what he wrote about her hands…

MY WIFE'S HANDS

~Her hands have so often ministered to my needs. So many times, and now for so many years, they have done the menial tasks of the homemaker, taking meticulous care of every detail about the house; the cleaning, laundering, decorating, arranging the furnishings with all those extra touches, making the home so perennially attractive, making sure that her husband can live in an atmosphere of comfort and relaxation. ~These hands, too, have provided so many delicious meals, arranging each detail at the table with professional finesse and yet with complete informality. So many meals, also, have her hands provided for our guests who in innumerable instances have been for the purpose of enhancing my happiness and promoting the interests of my work. And, oh, the tens of thousands of dishes, and pots and pans, and silverware these hands have washed.
~And the million little every day things her hands have done just for me. Even the exhilarating experience she grants me of simply holding her hands. What strength, reassurance, and inspiration I get from this! The countless times we have walked along together, hand in hand; and so many times, we have at night closed our eyes for sleep with our hands interlocked. And when I have been ill those hands attended me, and when I have been discouraged, those hands on my brow have dispelled my heartache.

~Those hands have ministered to the needs of my children. Nothing in all of life has been so inspiring as to see those loving hands care for those precious little ones, providing for their every comfort and necessity from changing diapers to spoon feeding them and tucking them in at night.

~In greeting friends, likewise, those hands have conveyed so much welcome and hospitality; and in clasping hands with them in a farewell- so much sincere and good will and friendship have been expressed.

~And oh, when her hands have so often been lifted up in prayer it has brought blessing to my heart; and no doubt the dear Lord in heaven has been gladdened because of the expression of those hands.

~Those soft, gentle hands, those hands of industry, those hands of hospitality, those hands of love - my wife's hands!

(published one year before she went to be with the Lord)

One day, ladies, our hands too, will be folded across our chests in death as we pass into eternity, done with our work on this earth. With opportunity gone, will you be pleased for all of eternity with your finished work, or will you have regrets to suffer? Will **all** your work have been accomplished with a willing heart? What will others remember as they pass by your casket and gaze upon your hands folded in completion of the tasks you were privileged to be responsible for? May we be able to one day hear the words of our Lord and family say, "Well done, thou good and faithful servant."

THE TREASURES OF THE VIRTUOUS WOMAN

Proverbs 31:14

"She is like the merchants' ships; she bringeth her food from afar."

Those merchants' ships the Bible speaks of were loaded with various kinds of merchandise - a heavy load to be sure! Yet, those ships held up under the weight of the load. In much the same way, the virtuous woman holds up under the load of responsibility for her household. She does not sink for thinking of carrying such a load, but rises to the occasion with the grace and beauty similar to the way those sturdy vessels glide across the sea with a splendor all their own. Though met with many a storm, these ships retained their usefulness with a determination to reach the goal for which it set out.... How are you doing carrying your load today, dear lady? Are you creaking with fatigue or sailing gaily along? Are you sinking after having met up with a storm in your life? May we all be steadfastly determined to hold up under the weight of our responsibilities! Let us not be rendered useless by the winds and rains that come during our journey here on earth.

Matthew 14:33, "Then they that were in the ship came and worshipped him, saying, Of a truth thou art the Son of God."

Every ship that has ever sailed, no matter how great in size, wouldn't dare leave the shore without its anchor, and so it is with the virtuous woman who always finds her security in the Lord. Ladies, our anchor does not lay in the deepest sea, but in the highest heaven. Jesus Christ is our unbending stabilizer when the going gets tough! "And it holds, my anchor holds...Blow your wildest then o' gale...On my bark so small and frail.... By His grace I shall not fail...For my anchor holds.... My anchor holds!!!"

Hebrews 6:19, "Which hope we have as an anchor of the soul, both sure and stedfast...."

Yes, those merchants' ships were filled with many treasures hidden away to the human eye - until they were unloaded one by one upon reaching their proper destination. Usually, there were many willing buyers anxiously awaiting the arrival of the ships that carried the needs and wants of those in waiting. Just like those merchants ships, a virtuous woman will also carry within her the treasures that she has gleaned from the Word of God to satisfy the various spiritual needs of her home. She realizes the importance of spiritual food – its strength and power, the wholesome nutrition her family will gain from such wise eating habits. She knows her loved ones will develop maturity upon consuming and swallowing every precious word in the Holy Bible. Jeremiah 15:16, "Thy words were found and I did eat them; and thy word was unto me the joy and rejoicing of mine heart..." The Word of God is health to the heart of every man and woman, and a virtuous woman will see to it that no matter how far she may have to travel to get the Word of God, the trip is worth it!!

How about you, dear lady? How do you personally feel about church involvement? Have you recognized the importance of getting into church **regularly**, regardless of the length of time it may take to get there?

A church alive is worth the drive! Are you bringing spiritual food home for your family, or are you making excuses for not seeking diligently after the true treasures in this life?

Hebrews 10:25, "Not forsaking the assembling of ourselves together, as the manner of some is; but exhorting one another: and so much the more, as ye see the day approaching."

In this passage above, the Word of God exhorts us to assemble together with other believers for the purpose of edification. We gain strength from one another; we stir up one another's faith, keep each other motivated to do right. The purpose for gathering together is for participation in worship of God and fellowship with one another. This cannot be done apart from assembling. You see, church is more than just a place to be entertained or a place to go just to hear the Word of God. If that is all you want, stay home and turn on the television - as the manner of some is! Today there is a growing movement of "home churches" where Christians are leaving the assembly of believers and gathering outside of the AUTHORITY of the local church, trying to set up their homes as a church, and themselves as their own authority. Scripture is quite clear as to the definition and qualifications of a local church.... Ladies, this behavior is born of a selfish and rebellious nature, an outward manifestation of the inward condition of the heart. The Lord tells us to gather for the sake of others, as well as for our own spiritual benefit. That means attendance of church is necessary - *whether you think so or not*! God clearly states that we ought to gather together SO MUCH THE MORE as we see the day of His coming approaching, not so much the less! It is not a time to scatter off on our own...
If your faith isn't taking you to church, how can you expect that it will get you to heaven?? Let us be found living lives of obedience in the light of the second coming of Christ!

A virtuous woman will not desert the local church. Moreover, she would never forsake authority over her life - as the manner of some also is! She obediently assembles to eat spiritual food AND to encourage others to persevere in their faith in the Lord.

Genesis 49:1&2a, "And Jacob called unto his sons, and said, Gather yourselves together, that I may tell you that which shall befall you in the last days. Gather yourselves together...."

Genesis 10:39, "For the children of Israel and the children of Levi shall bring the offering of the corn, of the new wine, and the oil, unto the chambers, where are the vessels of the sanctuary, and the priests that minister, and the porters, and the singers: and we will not forsake the house of our God."

So often, mothers will bring their children "treats" home from their shopping excursions, whether it be their favorite snack, or a new toy, or an article of clothing etc., never considering the importance of developing in them a Biblical appetite for the things of God. Do your concerns for your children extend further than this world? There is a great danger in this neglect as the story I have included below indicates...
~ A daughter came to a worldly mother and said she was anxious about her sins, and she had been praying all night. The mother said: "Oh, stop praying. I don't believe in praying. Get over all these religious notions, and I'll give you a dress that will cost $500, and you may wear it next week to that party." The daughter took the dress, and she moved in the gay circle, the gayest of the gay, that night. Sure enough, all religious impressions were gone, and she stopped praying. A few months after this, when she came to die, she said in her closing moments: "Mother, I wish you would bring me that dress which cost $500." The mother thought it a very strange request, but she brought it to please the dying child.

"Now," said the daughter, "Mother, hang that dress on the foot of my bed." The dress was hung there - on the foot of the bed. Then the dying girl got up on one elbow and looked at her mother. Pointing to the dress, she said: "Mother, that dress is the price of my soul." Oh, what a momentous thing it is to be a mother! ~

Ladies, may we by our own holy choices, create in our children a hearty appetite for heavenly things; a love for the Word of God, a love for the house of God, a love for the people of God, and a love for the lost soul. Such love ought to be stronger than a desire for the delicacies this world may have to offer them, amen?

Job 23:12, "Neither have I gone back from the commandment of his lips; I have esteemed the words of his mouth more than my necessary food."

Psalm 119:103, "How sweet are thy words unto my taste! yea, sweeter than honey to my mouth!"

Such a desire must first begin within our hearts... Think about how on payday, we set out eagerly for the mall, or Wal-mart, or maybe the nearest outlet for our bargains. We can't wait to see what treasures await us! I wonder though, is it that way when you open the Word of God? Is it that way when you're headed for church to hear a sermon? When you arrive at the house of God, are you only looking for what you can get, never considering what you can also give? When shopping, we *expect* to find a bargain and are more than willing to drive across the county for one, but what is our level of expectation when we open the Bible? We rarely look for treasures in the Word of God, and we certainly aren't as willing to drive any distance for truth like we will for a good deal on a furniture set!

Ladies, if we're honest with ourselves, we aren't even willing to spend a little extra time cross-referencing verses to learn of things spiritual - yet we will spend hours searching and sniffing out a promising garage sale! Yes, we'll take time to map out our travels in this world to bring home our earthly treasures, but we're lost when it comes finding anything in the Word of God... When is the last time you eagerly hunted for a *special treasure* within His Word? Scripture is loaded with true delights for our soul; we're just unwilling to put forth some effort to search them out! Best of all, God's treasures are free! What do you consider the BEST things? When compared to eternal blessings, what the world has to offer our soul is nothing more than trash. Bring some "food" home from afar, won't you? Carry some food straight from heaven so that you are equipped to meet the various needs of your family!

John 6:58, "This is that bread <u>which came down from heaven</u>: not as your fathers did eat manna, and are dead: he that eateth of this bread shall live for ever."

In summary, consider today whether you are faithfully feasting on the Word of God or just absorbing worldly nutrients. Many overweight Christian people today have stronger appetites for earthly food than for the Word of God! We love snacks, and I daresay your cupboards - like mine - are full of them. Do we think to snack on the Scriptures when that spare moment in our schedule turns up, or do we just reach for the Oreos and a cup of tea? What will it be for you, dear lady – ice cream sundaes or Sundays in church?

Let's be like those wonderful merchants ships mentioned in our opening verse today- filled with all the wonderful treasures we have found within the Word of God, and received while at the House of God, then bringing it all back into our homes to benefit our loved ones... Be willing too, to weather the storms you'll encounter in life and anchor yourself in the Lord Jesus Christ so that when you arrive on the other shore you will have no regrets!

THE AWAKENING OF THE VIRTUOUS WOMAN

Proverbs 31:15

This morning......zzzzzz.......we will be......zzzz...zz....looking at...zzzzz....verse 15....zzzz...of Proverbs 31......ZZZZZZZZ. Oh, excuse me, I must have dozed off for a second! It's so dark out.....zzz..... and it makes me.......zzzzz.....so sleepy..zz..zzzzzzz.... You understand don't you....?....zzzzzzzzz..... Just need a little... zzz..... more..zzzz ... sleep .....ZZZ

"She riseth also while it is yet night, and giveth meat to her household, and a portion to her maidens."

Yes, the virtuous woman is an *early riser*, ladies! She riseth while it is yet **D-A-R-K**. Hmm... What color is the sky when YOU finally rise? What do you think it is that motivates this woman to get up at what some would consider an "ungodly" hour? It is as the Bible states in the verse above - she riseth to give. Ladies, this unselfish woman forsakes spending the morning in bed and refuses to let her flesh dictate the hour of her rising! She is not the sort of woman who reaches for the alarm clock that just violated the fogginess of her precious sleep only to fling it across the room in aggravation. She has learned well the secret of rising up early and preparing herself *and* her household for the day that lies ahead. No doubt, she counted the cost the night before and even started *then* with preparing for the next day. With others on her mind, she fell asleep, and with others on her mind, she awakens. Who is the virtuous woman's role model in this matter of rising up early? It is Jesus Christ Himself....

Mark 1:35, "And in the morning, rising up a great while before day, he went out, and departed into a solitary place, and there prayed."

Ladies, the virtuous woman knows that Jesus is there waiting for her in the early hour and she willingly gets up to meet her Savior to have that special time in prayer and Bible reading. As a result, she can better face her family with a heart that is ready to sing and lips that are full of praise!

Psalm 57:7 & 8, "My heart is fixed, O God, my heart is fixed; I will sing and give praise. Awake up, my glory; awake, psaltery and harp: I myself will awake early."

Psalm 119:147, "I prevented the dawning of the morning, and cried: I hoped in thy word."

Perhaps if we looked as forward to meeting with the Lord we would awaken earlier too, for a proper relationship with the Lord makes getting up early a piece of cake! Some may say, "Well, I am a night owl" or "I'm not an early bird" and then roll over until their snoring subsides and their eyes decide for themselves when to open. However, we can see in light of scripture that early rising is a matter of the *heart* rather than heredity or personality. I hope you do not need someone to call you on the telephone just to get you out of bed, and I certainly hope you don't need someone to call you to remind you to read the precious Word of God! The condition of your heart should take care of *both* matters! You see ladies, the virtuous woman has filled herself with wisdom from the Word of God and has taken the scriptures to <u>heart</u>. Now they dictate her <u>life</u>! She remembers the words of the Lord Jesus in Acts 20:35 where He is quoted as saying, "It is more blessed to give than to receive."

The virtuous woman believes and acts upon the words that are hidden in her heart. Therefore, she is a giver at heart. Her heart is fixed and she desires to give above that of receiving. Sleep is a small sacrifice for her in light of meeting with her beloved Savior. Sleep is a small sacrifice for her in properly meeting the needs of her family as well... If crucifying her flesh is necessary to rise to a worthy occasion, then that is what a woman of virtue will do - *apart from whining about it*! Her heart dictates to her flesh what is important and makes a difference in her attitude altogether.

Isaiah 26:9, "With my soul have I desired thee in the night; yea, with my spirit within me will I seek thee early: for when thy judgments are in the earth, the inhabitants of the world will learn righteousness."

How about us, ladies? How are we doing in the area of early rising? Is this a weakness for you? Have you been snuggling up with those excuses of yours so that you can sleep a little longer? Do your children wake up to a mommy that has prepared her heart and mind for the day ahead by spending time in the Word of God and prayer? I have actually heard of mothers who have purchased VCR's just so their children can get up, watch television on their own, and not bother them while they sleep! Junior is left to the mercy of the television while mother snores away... He is sitting in bed cramming his little fist deep into a box of Cheerios for breakfast, while his impressionable mind 'breakfasts' on a movie rather than the example of a mother whose life demonstrates to him what is most important! God help us!! Gone almost, are the days when steaming hot oatmeal awaited little ones to hungrily devour it's nourishing warmth for breakfast - lovingly prepared by a mother who cared enough to rise up early to fix it!

Proverbs 19:15, "Slothfulness casteth into a deep sleep; and an idle soul shall suffer hunger."

My sister, who at one time volunteered her services at a nearby Christian school, shared with me that the quality of lunches children brought to school were appalling. One little six year old was given nothing more than two pieces of bundt cake in his lunch box! One kindergarten boy daily brought two frozen pieces of pizza wrapped in only a store grocery bag. Many children told her they were still hungry, or tried to take the lunches of the other children. One little fellow begged her not to give him any homework because his mommy is too tired to help him and gets mad. A little girl came to school sick one day and the school office called her mother to come get her who replied that she wouldn't because she was too tired and not feeling well herself! Can you imagine that??

Yes, in CHRISTIAN school, where one would assume the mothers are Christians or at least uphold proper values. The examples are too numerous to mention, but ladies, it's clear that many mothers are not thinking of nor preparing for their families the way God intended they should! We need the daily strength and wisdom the Lord has for us in His Word to carry out family responsibilities with the right heart attitude, amen? Our hearts must be fixed in a way that they can bring glory and honor to God and happiness to our children's hearts and our homes in general. It will not happen by accident, YOU must put forth the effort. YOU must purpose in your own heart to get up early and do right; nobody else can do that for you! The desire must be born within you.... Isn't your family worth it? Isn't the cause of Christ worth it??

Ecc. 10:18, "By much slothfulness the building decayeth; and through idleness of the hands the house droppeth through."

Has your husband just been getting a grunt from your side of the bed before he leaves for work in the morning, or is the memory of a warm hug from his wife given at the door carried with him throughout the day?
Can he pull out of the driveway and find you smiling and waving goodbye - even at an early hour - or aren't you found smiling until around noon? If it has been a while, why not rise up early and surprise your husband with a hearty breakfast for a change? Couple it with a kiss goodbye at the door before he leaves for the day. Take to heart what the virtuous woman has found to be true - it is more blessed to give than to receive! As you divide your time up wisely, God will multiply it! Don't sleep your blessings away, or squander the time that you could be utilizing to be a blessing to your family. Get up with a godly purpose....

Eccles. 3:1, "To every thing there is a season, and <u>a time to every purpose</u> under the heaven:"

Preparation is the purpose for which the virtuous woman rose early. Preparation first, of her heart… In so doing, she was able to give meat to her household and to her maidens, or for any others that she may have had responsibility. May I ask you what kind of meat you have prepared for your family today? Is it tough and chewy, dried out and stringy, flavorless, creating in them a loss of appetite? On the other hand, are you going to serve them meat that has been tenderized and marinated, mingled with oil and savory? The meat that I am referring to is *spiritual* meat, ladies. Did you know that meat offerings in the Old Testament were prepared in the morning and most always mingled with oil, that oil being a picture of the Holy Spirit? In Judges 14:14 the Bible says that "out of the eater came forth meat". If you are preparing your heart with the Word of God and eating of it's nourishment, out of *you* will come forth a portion of meat for your family. It will be meat marinated with the Holy Spirit and full of flavor, creating in your loved ones a healthy desire for the things of God!

Jeremiah:15:16 says, "Thy words were found and I did eat them; and thy word was unto me the joy and rejoicing of mine heart: for I am called by thy name, O Lord God of hosts."

Psalm 119:103, "How sweet are thy words unto my taste! yea, sweeter than honey to my mouth!"

You see, ladies, the virtuous woman realizes that *her* heart's appetite will greatly affect her home and all that goes on within it. We need to rise up early because of our own desire for the Word, not because someone gave us a call and reminded us to! This business of getting up early results from an <u>inward</u> influence, not an <u>outward</u> influence.

I don't know about you, but I usually wake up hungry every morning and prefer to eat right away. Nobody has to tell me to feed myself, I just do it! Likewise, it should be the same, spiritually speaking. Are you waking up hungry for a spiritual breakfast? Are you automatically reaching for the Word of God to feed your starving soul? After having consumed an adequate portion of truth, are you then turning around and giving to your family? I hope so, for their spiritual life and health depends upon it! You will be glad you did, or you will be sorrowful if you do not....

Job 6:7 says, "The things that my soul refused to touch are as my sorrowful meat."

Yes, life is tasteless and even loathsome without the Lord... Once again, in this matter of devotion to the Word of God, the example of the virtuous woman is Jesus Christ, and I hope He is yours as well. What was HIS meat? Look with me as we close with John 4:34....

"Jesus saith unto them, My meat is to do the will of him that sent me, and to finish his work."

Have you any such meat, dear lady? Let us not be guilty of neglecting the work the Lord has for each of us to do in our hearts and homes by trading it in for sleep. "Rise and Shine" to *give* to your household!

THE CONSIDERATIONS OF THE VIRTUOUS WOMAN

Proverbs 31:16, Part 1

Today we are going to dig deep into Proverbs 31:16, so get your Bible out and expect to find hidden treasure. Better bring a shovel along too! By the way, the *size* of your shovel will reveal the *size* of your expectation....

"She considereth a field, and buyeth it: with the fruit of her hands she planteth a vineyard."

There is much to uncover in this verse about the virtuous woman and we are going to begin by looking at the word "considereth". Webster's 1828 defines this word as: fixing the mind on; meditating on; pondering; viewing with care and attention; deliberating on. Ladies, these qualities are desperately lacking in people today… Who thinks anymore? Who ponders a thing? Who views anything with care and attention? Who deliberates over a situation? Sad to say, the only thing we fix our minds on most often is the television! Yes, common sense is uncommon - even among God's people. However, this is not so with a woman of virtue! She does not just look at the *surface* of matters as Eve hastily did in Genesis 3 when she foolishly took of the forbidden fruit. No, the virtuous woman looks *beyond* the surface appearance and views with care and careful attention the item or situation she is confronted with.

Within her mind dwells the ability to think things through wisely - she "considereth". Why? Because she does not want to suffer loss of any kind! Through wisdom found in the Word of God, a woman of virtue has discernment and exercises it before acting upon anything that is in her path. She is not hasty in spirit and therefore is not wasteful in nature, there are no desolate areas in her life. She wastes not - including her opportunities to advance her home and the kingdom of God.

Proverbs 21:5, "The thoughts of the diligent tend only to plenteousness; but of every one that is hasty only to want."

We read in our main verse today that the virtuous woman considereth a field, and *then* the Bible says she buyeth it. The virtuous woman did not procure anything apart from first counting the cost! Do we behave in such a cautious, sober minded manner? Why should we first count the cost of things? Let us turn to Luke 14:28 for the answer....

"For which of you, intending to build a tower, sitteth not down first, and counteth the cost, whether he have sufficient to finish it?"

Ladies, if we intend to make anything of our individual Christian lives, or our homes, we need to understand what it is going to take to see the thing through. That means we must first look at the value of what is at stake when we do take on something new in our lives.
So often, we are quick to jump into relationships, financial obligations, ministry obligations, work schedules etc. apart from considering whether the tower we are intending to build for God will ever be completed. To further elaborate this point, I'd like us to look at Matthew 13:44, so bring your shovel and follow me as we keep on digging for more wisdom from God's Word....

"Again, the kingdom of heaven is like unto treasure hid in a field; the which when a man hath found, he hideth, and for joy thereof goeth and selleth all that he hath, and buyeth that field."

As we apply this truth to the character of the virtuous woman, we come to understand that she considers matters in the light of eternity. Therefore, her ability to discern that there is treasure hid in a field comes after careful consideration of things eternal in comparison to things temporal. In other words, ladies, her priorities are in order! Hence, she takes on nothing new that will alter her priorities. (Ouch!) You see, the virtuous woman realizes that this world has nothing to offer her in the way of treasure, as does the kingdom of God. Have you personally realized that yet, or are you still tangled up with the world? The things of earth grow strangely dim in the light of God's glory and grace! Do not "buy into" what you first have not given a great deal of thought and prayer. To do so would be to gamble with your heart....

Matthew 6:21 says, "For where your treasure is, there will your heart be also."

Just where is your treasure today, dear lady? Wherever it is, start digging and you will find your heart buried there.... Is your heart buried in a career? Is your heart buried in an ungodly relationship? Is your heart buried in worldly activities? Is your heart buried in seeking wealth or fame? Is your heart buried in an accumulation of unnecessary responsibilities that you have taken on thoughtlessly? Where would we have to bury you should we determine the location of your heart today? Let me ask you this question: How do you determine the value of something? There is a difference between the *value* of something and the *price*, is there not?

To value something is to consider with respect its importance or worth, to esteem something highly. The price is what you pay for it; it's cost, the sum placed upon it. It is not the labor that makes things valuable, but their being valuable that makes them worth laboring for! So, what do you value today? I daresay it will be where your greatest labor is being put forth - where your shovel can be found digging daily... May we, as the virtuous woman does, place value on things eternal after careful consideration of what really matters most.

Isaiah 33:6 says, "And wisdom and knowledge shall be the stability of thy times, and strength of salvation: the fear of the Lord is his treasure."

Oh, that we could all say our treasure is with the fear of the Lord! I want us to look at verse 44 in Matthew 13 further. Scripture says that the kingdom of heaven is like unto treasure hid in a field. How so? Is it hid because we have not chosen to look for it? Is it hid to us because our eyes are blinded to it through wrong relationships, possessions, or personal ambitions that have distorted our view of the field that lies before us? Is it hid by God?? Today let us search our hearts and spend some time considering the field that lies before each one of us wherever we are located. Let us ask God to help us find the treasure He has for us that may be hid to us today due to poor management. Perhaps you haven't been interested in getting "dirty" in the service of the Lord; you don't like working around lost souls. Maybe you've left your shovel somewhere in the world and forgotten where you last put it... Whatever it takes, get it out again and get busy digging for treasure in *your* field! In this day and age, we prefer bulldozers to shovels, don't we? Anything faster, which requires less effort and not as much perspiration, sounds great to us!

Nevertheless, ladies, God uncovers things to us one shovelful at a time and knows that we are strengthened by the labor. You will not find your treasure anywhere else but in YOUR own field, within your own sphere of influence. It is not hiding at my house, at your friend's house, or at your mother's house - it's right under your very own nose!

Col. 3:3b, "...and your life is hid with Christ in God."

Now, how does the Bible say this man in Matthew 13:44 felt when his treasure was uncovered? Scripture says – "and for joy". Yes, he was *joyful* even after the labor required to find it! So too, the virtuous woman experiences joy after first considering a field before buying it, and then working faithfully in what she has taken on. Those of you who are married have taken on a husband, probably children too. Are you faithful in taking good care of them? This is what adds extra value to your field on top of it's already realized eternal value! Ladies, have you been trying to find joy some other way in your life, apart from faithfulness to that which matters most? Joy is found accompanying the treasure that lies waiting for you in your field - your **home** - through going about your work willingly and diligently, filled with compassion rather than compulsion.

Haggai 1:7, "Thus saith the Lord of hosts; Consider your ways."

No doubt about it, building a tower and finishing it requires self sacrifice. In turn, self-sacrifice brings sharper eyesight, enhancing our vision and placing our focus on things eternal. As we die to self, we are no longer blinded by the temporal. With her heart given to her heavenly Father, and her hand given to others, the virtuous woman enjoyed a life that was completely unselfish.

She found treasure that had been hidden simply by taking the time to "considereth a field." Has the devil kept you so busy, dear lady, that you don't have time to consider your life - your field - and the path it is taking? Don't let the enemy clutter your mind and keep you from uncovering the highest priorities. Take the time to CONSIDER what lies right under your nose. Then go one step further - BUY IT! All you have to do is die to self to claim it… What sacrifices are you willing to make in order to fully embrace Christ and His kingdom? Consider the cost… Is giving it all too high a price for you? You cannot buy *your field* any other way - you have to sell out first!

THE PRODUCE OF THE VIRTUOUS WOMAN

Proverbs 31:16, Part 2

I hope you remember where you put your shovel after we went treasure hunting in the scriptures yesterday, because today we need to go back out into the field and look at the second part of verse 16 of Proverbs 31, and the life of the virtuous woman....

"She considereth a field, and buyeth it: with the fruit of her

hands she planteth a vineyard."

Notice the colon in the middle of this verse. This causes us to pause and reflect on the first part of the verse and then prepare to contrast the second part along with it. The field has been purchased, the virtuous woman has sold-out for her Lord and Savior - now what? Now is the time for work! She rolls up her sleeves, takes that field where her treasure and her joy is cultivated and "with the fruit of her hands" planteth a vineyard. What does the fruit of her hands mean? I like to think it is a picture of those that this woman has personally discipled in the Lord, probably even led to Christ herself. Is there any fruit to our hands today in this area of soul winning and discipling others? When the things of eternity become a priority in our lives, souls will be precious to us! Titus 2 exhorts women to be "teachers of good things". That means we have to bring people to Christ so we can teach them! Otherwise, we have nobody to share the truths of God's Word with…

Luke 14:23, " And the lord said unto the servant, Go out into the highways and hedges, and compel them to come in, that my house may be filled."

Ladies, I hope that there is at least *one* woman that you are responsible for teaching and training to labor in the field God has provided them at salvation....

2 Tim. 2:2, "And the things that thou hast heard of me among many witnesses, the same commit thou to faithful men, who shall be able to teach others also."

One thing you must know; the virtuous woman is not a one-man band. She does not have to be the boss or the top dog who runs the show all the time but can work well with others. She is not concerned with whether or not she shines brightest. This is not the motivation for her work; it is simply a result of the pureness of her life. Today in many Bible-believing churches, there are Christians who cannot work well together in the field of the Lord Jesus Christ for one shallow reason or another. What a pity we cannot be content just to work along side of one another for the cause of Christ without having to be the one "in charge" all the time! You see ladies, the virtuous woman, while working with others, realizes that it may mean more of dying to herself, for the WORK is her priority, not her position of power. She is content to lead by example in the field and be sure that HER hands are always producing fruit. She does not stop production to feel sorry for herself and begin pouting for going unnoticed. How does she do it? She has hidden in her heart the Word of God. The Lord Jesus Christ is her 'boss'; the One who gives her the proper perspective on her work in the field, herself and others.

1 Corinthians 3:7, "So then neither is he that planteth any thing, neither he that watereth; but God that giveth the increase."

Yes, humility always gets the job done without complaint! How about you, dear lady? Have you recently dropped your shovel and taken a break from digging in the field of the Lord? Have you been found complaining of the way things are or are not being done in your church? Is your complaining testimony a distraction to the Lord's work? Have people had to stop serving the Lord just to cater to your whining, just to quiet you like a spoiled infant? What a waste of valuable time!

Psalm 55:2, "Attend unto me, and hear me: I mourn in my complaint, and make a noise;"

Better bite your tongue ma'am, and get back to the work, for time is running out, eternity is just around the corner! Be careful you are not the reason that other laborers throw in their shovels and quit simply because you have sown seeds of discouragement while working along side of them! It's a pleasure to work with someone who has a song in his or her heart. Why don't you shine forth as that one? John 4:36 says that he that soweth and he that reapeth are going to one day rejoice together for all of eternity, why not get along with one another now?

The next thing I see about the virtuous woman in this half of the verse is that she is a planter, not a destroyer. She is a seed-sower. That means she enjoys seeing growth, not hindering it. Those of you who have gardens know the satisfaction such a work can bring. Daily you visit your garden to check for abundant life and spy out any new weeds that may have cropped up. Do you get as much satisfaction out of seeing souls saved and witnessing spiritual growth as it springs up in new converts lives? Are you as diligent about checking up on those babes in Christ as you are at spying out the new weeds in your garden? As soon as a weed is spotted, we stomp over to it and extract the intruder with a certain air of steadfast determination and protection over the crops that we have labored to plant. Yet, our hearts are indifferent toward that new believer who may be struggling in their walk with the Lord. Hence, we never personally assist in their discipleship. We take better care of produce than we do people! Perhaps someone you have been neglecting needs closer tending to...

Galatians 6:1, "Brethren, if a man be overtaken in a fault, ye which are spiritual, restore such an one in the spirit of meekness; considering thyself, lest thou also be tempted."

What would a virtuous woman desire to plant in her field? How does she go about making such a decision? Yesterday we studied the fact that a woman of virtue *considereth* the field before buying it; paying careful attention to it, meditating on it, fixing her mind on it, viewing it, pondering it etc. She looks *ahead* to the end of things. To do so helps us to wisely plant today! I think perhaps what we read below in Proverbs 24:30-32, was also part of her consideration before the virtuous woman began planting. An entry in her diary may have read something like these scriptures:

"I went by the field of the slothful, and by the vineyard of the man void of understanding; and, lo, it was all grown over with thorns, and nettles had covered the face thereof, and the stone wall thereof was broken down. Then I saw, and considered it well: I looked upon it, and received instruction."

I can picture the virtuous woman dropping to her knees at the sight of such a desolate field and in tears asking God to prevent such a thing from happening to her field, humbly crying out to Him for wisdom to plant wisely. Do you see why we need to CONSIDER things, ladies? For in so doing we learn and can then apply our hearts to wisdom! We can determine that which is best to plant and that which is not. We can also protect our homes, lives, and prevent desolation occurring in our field. We are to soberly consider the result of planting wrong seeds....

Proverbs 21:12, "The righteous man considereth the house of the wicked...."

Yes, the Bible says that instruction was received from just *seeing* such a field! Ladies, are you and I that teachable today? May God help us to be! Why would we want to live in such a way as to be void of understanding and have our lives end up as the description of the field of the slothful?

Are you determined to prosper spiritually or go on living a life void of understanding? What kind of seeds are you planting today in your field? Yes, the Bible says that instruction was received from just *seeing* such a field! Ladies, are you and I that teachable today? May God help us to be! Why would we want to live in such a way as to be void of understanding and have our lives end up as the description of the field of the slothful? Are you determined to prosper spiritually or go on living a life void of understanding? What kind of seeds are you planting today in your field? I hope you will take some time to consider what you intend to produce. The virtuous woman planted a vineyard - life in which Jesus Christ was her focus. It's the only way to achieve success in your labors!

John 15:4-5, "Abide in me, and I in you. As the branch cannot bear fruit of itself, except it abide in the vine; no more can ye, except ye abide in me. I am the vine, ye are the branches: He that abideth in me, and I in him, the same bringeth forth much fruit: for without me ye can do nothing."

That which the virtuous woman produced was agreeable to the Spirit of God. Her words, her actions, her thoughts, her affections etc. were of the nature of Christ. So dear lady, is your planting yielding forth the peaceable fruit of righteousness or is your field all grown over with thorns and nettles? In studying out thorns and nettles there is much to learn. Thorns were a curse given by God to Adam's garden in Genesis 3:17 & 18. That is their beginning. They were a result of his disobedience. Are there areas in your life that you know are in direct disobedience to God and His Word? You are growing thorns! In Mt. 13:7, thorns are found growing in shallow, stony ground. Is that a description of your heart today?

We all know a crown of thorns was placed upon the head of Jesus Christ as shown in Mt. 27:29. Think of that...all our disobediences placed upon our King's head for a crown to wear and then the pain of that disobedience felt sharply as the crown was driven into his skull! Our Savior deserves to find better than that of us growing in our fields! In Hebrews 6:7 & 8, the fate of thorns is mentioned as ending up being burned. I hope that we are taking care not to grow thorns in our fields, only to find one day that all our works will be burned....

1 Cor. 3:15, "If any man's work shall be burned, he shall suffer loss..."

Nettles are a picture of desolation and barrenness. They usually grow in an abandoned field, where no sign of life is. Proverbs 24:31 says that, "nettles covered the face thereof". What does your face look like today? Does it reflect sobriety or foolishness; holiness or worldliness? Does it reflect joy because of the treasure you have found in selling out and serving the Lord, or does your countenance reflect a heart that is desolate, empty of joy, and filled with the bitterness that comes from a self-centered life? Ladies, your countenance is a mirror of your heart. You can *say* what you want, but others will *see* what is dwelling within you! Wisdom of heart shines forth on the face and is a beautiful sight.... No amount of cosmetics you and I use could ever create such a godly glow!

1 Samuel 25:3, " Now the name of the man was Nabal; and the name of his wife Abigail: and she was a woman of good understanding, and of a beautiful countenance...."

In closing, let us look at what to plant in our fields to prevent such desolation and barrenness from ever occurring. In 1 Peter 1:5-8 we will find the "seeds" listed that we need to sow:
 "And beside this, giving all diligence, add to your faith virtue; and to virtue knowledge; and to knowledge temperance; and to temperance patience; and to patience godliness; and to godliness brotherly kindness; and to brotherly kindness charity. For if these things be in you and abound, they make you that ye shall neither be barren nor unfruitful in the knowledge of our Lord Jesus Christ."

Perhaps you can see why the virtuous woman would drop to her knees in tears as she realized that all this fruit was missing from the field of the slothful. I hope this bountiful crop is not missing from our fields today! Maybe you have sown some of these precious, holy seeds already. Praise God for wise planting! With the Lord, there is no reason we ought ever to be barren, amen? With careful consideration and all diligence, keep planting and adding the right produce to your field so that thorns and nettles do not overtake it. Fill your field with righteousness! Cultivate that which stems from the True Vine.

THE STRENGTH OF THE VIRTUOUS WOMAN

Proverbs 31:17

"She girdeth her loins with strength, and strengtheneth her arms."

Planting a vineyard is definitely hard work and physical strength is certainly going to be necessary to get the job done. How is your physical strength doing today, dear lady? Are you always tired, worn out and easily frazzled? Are you taking proper care of your temple? Are you equipping yourself with the necessary strength for working in the field the Lord has given you? We need to be sure that we eat wisely and get a sufficient amount of rest (no more - no less!) so that we can carry out the work of the Lord - not only in our homes, but outside of them as well. How can you and I possibly endure a lifetime of work if we are daily abusing our bodies? Many Christians are not capable of much physical labor for the Lord for reason of being so out of shape. There is a growing number of God's people who are overweight and limited in their capabilities because of the extra pounds they are carrying. Many are continuously sick with one illness or another, and are greatly hindered because of their weak immune systems. Sad to say, but we probably wouldn't last long on a mission field in a foreign country in such sorry shape! Ladies, let's fortify ourselves with physical strength so that we can adequately accomplish the daily duties we need to carry out in our homes, our churches, and in the lives of others as we reach out and minister to them! Grace and health ought to be companions within us... A strong soul may be lodged in a weak body, and what can then be accomplished for God if this be the case? Those who have flourishing souls should also have healthful bodies so that there is still more room in their lives for activity on the Lord's behalf...

3 John 1:2, "Beloved, I wish above all things that thou mayest prosper and be in health, even as thy soul prospereth."

I read recently via e-mail of an overweight woman who had asked for prayer to be able to just clean her bathrooms that day! Her weight was limiting her from fulfilling even the smallest of household duties and her husband, upon returning home from a full day's worth of work, was having to clean their home as well. Ladies, our spouses need us to be strong enough to be able to work along side of them and be help meets that have some **endurance**! Do not be the cause for bringing your husband to the place of being ashamed of you. Make him proud of you! I think of Caroline Ingolls of "Little House on the Prairie" and how diligently she worked side by side with her husband Charles to build a homestead for their family. How he must have been thankful for a wife that could assist him in such a way. Consider all the physical labor alone that went into what they had to accomplish each day just in their normal responsibilities. I daresay that many of us would whine and collapse under such tasks if required of us today! Yes, the virtuous woman understands that *strength* is an important part of survival, and she takes responsibility to equip herself with plenty of it.

1 Cor. 6:19 & 20 says, "What? Know ye not that your body is the temple of the Holy Ghost which is in you, which ye have of God, and ye are not your own? For ye are bought with a price: therefore glorify God in your body, and in your spirit, which are God's."

Ladies, we can honor God with our bodies in many ways and physical strength is key to doing so. As I said a moment ago, what weak, sickly, or overweight Christian or missionary do you think is going to survive very long in the field? Don't you want to be able to hold up under the physical labor, the stress that living in this world brings upon us, and do so for the glory of God? You and I have been bought with a high price. That means we have been purchased to get an important, strenuous job done!

Romans 15:1, "We then that are strong ought to bear the infirmities of the weak...."

How many of us appreciate spending our hard earned money on a particular piece of equipment only to discover it doesn't function properly enough to get the job done for which it was purchased? It's a bit frustrating and discouraging, amen? Let us then give God our best when it comes to the physical function of our bodies! Are you increasing in your ability to bear infirmities, or is your tolerance waning? Be faithful to strengthen your temple so that you are capable of bearing up under the weight the Lord has proportioned for you.

Isaiah 25:3, "Therefore shall the strong people glorify thee...."

Proverbs 24:5, "A wise man is strong; yea, a man of knowledge increaseth strength."

Just as physical strength is important in our service to the Lord, so too is spiritual strength. Because the virtuous woman has her priorities in order, she recognizes the importance of strengthening herself in preparation for the spiritual battles she knows she will face in her field. Are you taking to heart the condition of your spiritual strength, dear lady? It is important to tend to the needs of others, but in order to do so effectively, we must be capable of carrying such a load ourselves, and apart from spiritual strength, we will not be able to do so! A woman of virtue strengtheneth her *arms* because she realizes that they are the support system to her hands, those little members of her body that will carry out the many acts of service and love both in her home and outside of her home. There is nothing so draining as spiritual warfare and we must increase in spiritual strength as the battle rages. Are you certain you're strong enough to shoulder the load??

Jeremiah 48:14, "How say ye, We are mighty and strong men for the war?"

Just as proper food, exercise and sleep are sources of physical strength; we also have sources of spiritual strength to draw from. That source is the Lord God Himself and His Word!

In Psalm 93:1 the Bible says, "... the Lord is clothed with strength, wherewith he hath girded himself..."

Psalm 96:6 says, "Honor and majesty are before him: strength and beauty are in his sanctuary."

Ladies, when we gird up our loins with strength from attendance upon the Word of God and attendance in the house of God, we are strengthening our arms to be able to serve Him victoriously in the field! Have you found yourself victorious in the day of battle, or easily overtaken by your enemies? Proverbs 24:10 says, "If thou faint in the day of adversity, thy strength is small." Should we be content with a small amount of strength? Certainly not! When our Lord returns, let us be found standing - not fainting! Ephesians 6:10 says, "Finally, my brethren, be strong in the Lord and in the power of His might." Perhaps the reason you have been fainting is that you are facing spiritual battles in your own strength and not in the Lord's! Ladies, the very weaknesses you and I were designed with are for knowing the strength of the Lord! Did you realize that? We curse God, and even ourselves for the times when we are weak and in so doing, never learn to draw upon Him for His strength to replace our weaknesses. This is the Biblical exercise program to achieving true strength!

2 Cor. 12:9 & 10 says, "And he said unto me, My grace is sufficient for thee: for my strength is made perfect in weakness. Most gladly therefore will I rather glory in my infirmities, that the power of Christ upon me. Therefore I take pleasure in infirmities, in reproaches, in necessities, in persecutions, in distresses for Christ's sake: for when I am weak, then am I strong."

ι encouraging portion of scripture! There is no need for us to allow the devil to beat us up for our weaknesses any longer. They are designed by the hand of a loving God to draw you and I into a closer fellowship with Him - a fellowship founded in His strength. Think for a moment of that one area that you are continually weak in.... If it were not there, would you still be drawing near to the Lord? I know I would not! I would move on in my own strength and leave God behind – not to mention forsaking the opportunities to increase my strength… Are you thankful for your weaknesses or do you resent having any at all, possibly even embarrassed by them? Do not let pride stand in the way of experiencing God's strength in your life. You see, ladies, God does not need our strength, we need His! The virtuous woman admits her weaknesses, accepts them, and girds up her loins for the work and for the battle with the strength of her Lord. She humbly trades in her weaknesses for His strengths and gets the job done for her Savior. Will you do the same?

1 Peter 1:13 says, "Wherefore gird up the loins of your mind, be sober, and hope to the end for the grace that is to be brought unto you at the revelation of Jesus Christ."

Our minds are where many battles are fought and won… The very source of our strength, the Word of God, exhorts us to gird up the loins of our mind.

If you cross reference the above scripture with Ephesians 6:14, which says, "Stand therefore, having your loins girt about with truth, and having on the breastplate of righteousness", you will notice that we need *truth* for strength in the day of battle. I don't have to remind you that the devil is a liar and the father of lies, do I? We are made weak by swallowing his lies, just as Eve did in the Garden of Eden. To gird is to surround. Is every area of your heart and mind surrounded with *truth* so that you can properly resist the devil and effectively guard yourself against his deceptive tactics? Yes, truth brings strength in the day of adversity and sets us free from our enemies!

In closing, may we tap into the secret of the virtuous woman's source of strength, as we look daily to the Lord and His Word. Let's prepare ourselves both physically and spiritually for the work that each of us has been called to do. Glorify God in your body *and* in your spirit…

2 Chron. 15:7, "Be ye strong therefore, and let not your hands be weak: for your work shall be rewarded."

THE PERCEPTION OF THE VIRTUOUS WOMAN

Proverbs 31:18, Part 1

"She perceiveth that her merchandise is good: her candle goeth not out by night."

The word "perceiveth" is defined as: known by the senses, felt, understood, and observed. Yes, the virtuous woman is keenly aware of the state of affairs going on around her - the well being of that which is in her care. She stands back and observes the lay of the land.... She regularly takes inventory of her merchandise to see if there comes up any lack. This check is not carried out for prideful reasons, but that she might bring that which turns up deficient back to a goodly - and godly - state. Wise is the woman who asks the Lord to help her see things through HIS eyes and not her own.... This is *true* perception!

Deut. 11:12, "A land which the Lord thy God careth for: the eyes of the Lord thy God are always upon it, from the beginning of the year even unto the end of the year."

Where then, would a virtuous woman begin her eagle-eyed inspection? Knowing what we do about her priorities so far, no doubt she checks to see if there is anything that needs to be added to her **home** to make it more comfortable, or that would cause it to run more efficiently. Is there a lamp needed for that corner of the room? Is there a rug needed by that door? Are storage containers necessary? She makes a list of new items that may need to be saved for and then purchased. Not only does she *add* to her home, the virtuous woman also *subtracts* from it... She "spring cleans" and gets rid of the junk that is cluttering closets, cupboards, and drawers and reorganizes **often**. Yes, quality is important to her and is not something she compromises.... She replaces the "old" towels that have become worn to transparency with new ones that her family can use and that will uphold! She notices when "Junior" needs new shoes or clothes BEFORE they no longer fit him. She is mindful of when her husband needs his suits taken to the cleaners, a missing button sewn on, or broken zipper repaired.

She takes heed to whether or not his shirts need ironing or his shoes need polishing. Yes, even the shine on his shoes doesn't pass her perceptive eye! She also observes when the paint, either inside or out, might need a fresh coat applied. Ladies, there isn't a cobweb that survives in any corner of the home of a virtuous woman for she spies it out from across the room! This gal even makes sure that there is toilet paper available when the current roll runs out, extra shoelaces on hand for those that would break, a back-up can of shaving cream stocked for her husband, necessary ingredients furnished for a variety of recipes - you name it and this woman has thought of it! If you can't find something, just ask the virtuous woman and she knows right where it is. "A place for everything and everything in its place" is her motto. She is highly in tune to what would best attend to the needs of those she serves in her home and *diligently* obtains the necessary "merchandise" in order to carry out her duties with forethought.

After reading these few examples given above, you might be thinking that your head would start spinning to be consumed with such minor details. Perhaps you may have already decided within yourself that they don't really matter, or that this is behavior typical of those "Martha Stewart" types who came to earth from another planet; but ladies, they **DO** matter! Put down the books you've been reading that justify you being "messy" in personality and pick up the **BIBLE** and read it! Regardless of who we are, as women, it is our God given responsibility to carefully **observe** what is going on in our homes! We are to be faithful in the little things as well as the big ones...

Luke 16:10, "He that is faithful in that which is least is faithful also in much: and he that is unjust in the least is unjust also in much."

You see, the virtuous woman's **heart** is in her home and as a result, ladies, so is her **head**! Her thoughts are naturally directed toward the guiding of her home because her heart has been planted there. Hence, whatever she puts her hands to ends up in a quality job well done, and *lovingly* done. It is important to a woman of virtue that what she does is her best because her family deserves it! Her feelings do not get in the way of a quality performance in the running of her household. In fact, she even takes regular inventory of her own daily attitudes and makes sure that they are in a goodly and godly state as well! Sharp perception is not hindered by self-centeredness or self-pity, but rather motivated by a heart bent on serving others. Due to <u>regular</u> examination of her merchandise, every little detail that goes on within the home of a virtuous woman is mentally documented. Therefore, deficiencies are caught in a timely fashion by her discerning eye and she makes note to address them promptly. Through good stewardship of her time, talents, and money, obtaining any necessary items is not a financial impossibility. As we read in earlier studies in Proverbs 21:5, the Bible says the thoughts of the diligent tend only to plenteousness, remember?

So, how are YOU doing today in this area of perception, dear lady? Are you getting a little lax on the overseeing of the "merchandise" placed in your care by the Lord? Have you neglected the task of taking inventory of such things because you haven't "felt" like it? Is your heart just not in your home anymore? Been a little to wrapped up in self, maybe? Been too busy outside of your home, perhaps??

1 Timothy 5:13 & 14 says, "And withal they learn to be idle, wandering about from house to house; and not only idle, but tattlers also and busybodies, speaking things which they ought not. I will therefore that the younger women marry, bear children, <u>guide the house</u>, give none occasion to the adversary to speak reproachfully."

Ladies, we ought to take this matter of guiding our homes seriously because we are to be orderly testimonies in a disorderly world. The world (and the church!) needs godly, orderly homes today more than ever before! Homes where the name of the Lord is upheld ought to shine brighter than worldly homes. Women can't guide the house properly if they're never home to consider what's going on! Might I add too, ladies, that the virtuous woman guides the affairs of her OWN home and does not become a busybody in the affairs of another! Such behavior can warp your perception of your own home... Many women have LEARNED to be idle by hanging out with other idle, purposeless women. Through the numerous distractions they fall prey to, idle women end up bankrupt in understanding how to guide their own homes. As a result, these silly women end up in ungodly conversations and unprofitable relationships at the expense of the decaying of their own families. Such an ill run home provides an occasion for others to speak reproachfully of the Lord Jesus Christ, Christians, and Christianity in general. Convincing themselves they are involved in a good work, many of God's people spend larger amounts of time building the homes of other people simply because it's easier and less stressful than constructing their own! However, good is not better than best... Ask God for a **heart** for your own home! Ask God to open your eyes to the things that need tending to in YOUR home that perhaps you have been blinded to or neglectful of. Ask Him for the wisdom, creativity, and *desire* (heart) in the overseeing of your merchandise so that you can perceive that it is good and quickly restore that which is deficient. A goodly state is that which the Lord expects to find your home in! But will He?? No matter what may be hidden to man's eyes, the Lord doesn't miss a thing.... He knows where your heart *really* is!

Proverbs 5:21, "For the ways of man are before the eyes of the Lord, and he pondereth all his goings."

One other point that I want to make here is that the virtuous woman is also perceptive to the spiritual and emotional state of affairs within her home. How is your marriage doing? Have you perceived a problem or a strain there? What are you going to do about seeing to it that it is good and that it stays good? Have you been tending to the things that would produce a healthy and happy relationship with your husband? How are your children doing emotionally, spiritually, academically? Are you observing any struggles or attitudes in certain areas of their lives that need tending to? Are you taking these concerns to the Lord in prayer on behalf of your family? Are you readjusting your schedule to give proper attention to the lack that has been identified? Ladies, a virtuous woman perceives even the inner struggles that are going on in her home and becomes a mediator on behalf of her loved ones as well as doing all she can to aid the beloved members of her family. They come first before all others… She works at restoring each individual to a goodly and a godly state, for their hearts are *precious merchandise* to her, and she knows they are precious to the Lord who entrusted her with the specific care of them.

Titus 2:5, "To be discreet, chaste, <u>keepers at home</u>, good, obedient to their own husbands, that the word of God be not blasphemed."

Tomorrow we will look at the second half of this verse but in the meantime, why not take some time to take inventory of the state of affairs in YOUR home. Observe the merchandise at your house and see to it that it is **good**!

THE RATIONALE OF THE VIRTUOUS
WOMAN Proverbs 31:18, Part 2

"She perceiveth that her merchandise is good: <u>her candle goeth not out by night</u>."

Her candle...What is the candle that belongs to a woman of virtue?

In Proverbs 20:27, the Bible says, "The spirit of man is the candle of the Lord, searching all the inward parts of the belly."

Yes, the Lord is the spirit, or the the candle that sheds light on the thoughts and intents of every woman's heart, traveling into all the places that no man can see - those deep, dark places that are hidden - at times even to ourselves....

Psalm 18:28, "For thou wilt light my candle: the Lord my God will enlighten my darkness."

The virtuous woman is thankful for such inner light and guidance, and the attitude of her heart is as verse 2 of Psalm 26 puts it; "Examine me, O Lord, and prove me; try my reins and my heart." To bring God's reasoning into the picture preserves us from absurdity... The question is, how teachable are OUR hearts when the Word of God is open before us? How willing are you to be examined, proven, and tried by truth? Do you allow the Word of God to thoroughly scrutinize you; do you measure yourself with "thus saith the Lord " rather than distorted reasoning? 2 Cor. 10:12-18 exhorts us to be careful of this type of examination of ourselves. What rationale are you using to measure yourself as a woman of God? Is it consistent with scripture?

The Bible teaches "they that compare themselves amongst themselves are not wise". It further conforms our reasoning by stating, "For not he that commendeth himself is approved, but whom the Lord commendeth." *You* may consider yourself a Proverbs 31 woman in comparison to others, but what would God consider you? Have you been extravagant in your rationale by patting yourself on the back a little too much? Ladies, let us be careful to allow the *Word of God* to enlighten our darkness and illuminate those specific areas each of us has matured in, and still needs to mature in! To pursue a course of irrationality is to travel the path that destroys true peace and happiness. It is that spiritual light, the candle of God glowing within her, that gives the virtuous woman the insight to perceive that the merchandise of her home, and those precious hearts of her loved ones, are doing well. Truth lights every step of the way in helping a woman of virtue to guide the affairs of her heart, as well as the affairs of her home. A woman yielding to the guidance of the Spirit of God brings a warm glow that surrounds those closest to her…

Mt. 5:15 says, "Neither do men light a candle, and put it under a bushel, but on a candlestick; and it giveth light unto all that are in the house."

How are you doing in your HOME, dear lady? Are you a glowing testimony to all that are in your house, or is your light covered today with the bushel of complaining, sin, laziness, negligence, bad attitudes, impatience, indifference etc. Are you typically rational in behavior or irrational? Do you become extremely upset over the least little situation or does the power of understanding permeate your soul? So often, we give our "glowing side" to those outside of our home while our loved ones receive just a little flicker of light now and again. Ladies, we must first reflect the Lord *at home*…

Luke 8:16 says, "No man, when he hath lighted a candle, covereth it with a vessel, or putteth it under a bed; but setteth it on a candlestick, that they which enter in may see the light."

When we are glowing within, there will be a difference seen in us of others. Nothing will be able to block that heavenly glow! Not even the darkness of a storm or a trial will send us over the edge.... Light bulbs burn out, but ladies, there is no reason for a *godly* light to ever burn out if we are tapping into the power of the Lord! We have one up on Thomas Edison! :-) Would you say you are "burned out" these days? Would you say you are hiding your Christianity in any way at all? Has a trial put out your light? What about your family as a unit... Is it a shining testimony for the Lord? When others enter your home, can they tell by the way that it is run that the Lord is the Light of your lives? Do you do things on a whim, or exhibit sound rationale? Is your home life one that God would have others to pattern themselves after? Are the godly conversations within your home such that they will be remembered long after your guests have left? Ladies, we can have a transforming affect upon those living within our homes as well as those that enter as guests. It's time to check and see how brightly your candle is glowing – or if it's gone out! Her candle goeth not out by night.... How hard are you willing to work to see to it that your merchandise is good? The virtuous woman often times has to work into the night to tend to the tasks that may need finishing. It does not mean, however, that she stays up late working into the wee hours of the morning simply because she wasted the day away in front of the television watching soap operas! No, a woman of virtue does not misappropriate her time during the day but rather uses the extra time at night *only if necessary.* She will do whatever she has to do to make sure that her home runs well even if it means losing an hour or two of sleep to do so!

This would not be too much to ask or expect of her. The virtuous woman willingly sacrifices her personal time if it means that her home will benefit.

Luke 2:8, "And there were in the same country shepherds abiding in the field, keeping watch over their flock by night."

Much like the shepherds spoken of above, the virtuous woman protectively watches over her flock by night tending also to the spiritual needs of her family. Ladies, have you ever thought to stay up an extra hour in the evening just to pray for your husband and children? When the closing of the day comes upon us and the darkness surrounds us, it can make our troubles and cares seem larger. Why not take your overwhelming concerns to the Lord before you lay your head down to sleep? Allow Him to shed His candle of understanding upon these situations and enhance your perception, while melting your worries away. Our God is always there at any hour of the night to take them from us! As you reflect upon the day and all that transpired, you may find that you are heavy hearted for a certain member of your family you sense may be wandering from the fold, perhaps in developing an attitude that needs repenting of - perhaps even YOU! Strange, but we'll refuse to go to bed until that last load of laundry is washed and folded, yet there are times when we have no problem at all tucking ourselves in to bed while harboring ill feelings towards our husbands and sleeping with *spiritually* dirty laundry! It makes no sense! It isn't *rational*... Know why? Because we've snuffed out the candle of the Lord by ignoring the still small voice of the Holy Spirit. May God help us to be as concerned over spiritual matters as we are our housework and getting it accomplished!

Certainly, repentance and restoration is worth staying up for, amen? Consider your rationale, dear lady... Are you more upset over the toys your children didn't pick up or the Bible they didn't pick up and read that day?? The principles leading you will become that which you practice! Let God speak sound reasoning to you so that your judgement may be right and *bright*...

Luke 11:34-36 says, "The light of the body is the eye: therefore when thine eye is single, thy whole body also is full of light; but when thine eye is evil, thy body also is full of darkness. Take heed therefore that the light which is in thee be not darkness. If thy whole body therefore be full of light, having no part dark, the whole shall be full of light, as when the bright shining of a candle doth give thee light."

In closing, I'd like to leave you with the thoughts of this poem:

You did not light its glow....
'Twas given you by other hands you know.

'Tis yours to keep it burning bright!
Yours to pass on when you no more need light...

For there are other feet that we must guide
And other forms go marching by our side:

Their eyes are watching every tear and smile,
And efforts which we think are not worthwhile-

Are sometimes just the very help they need,
Actions to which their souls would give most heed:

So that in turn they'll hold it high and say:
"I watched someone else carry it this way."

I think it started down it's pathway bright
The day the Maker said, "Let there be light."

And He once said, Who hung on Calvary's tree,
"Ye are the light of the world...Go shine for me."

THE COMPLIANCE OF THE VIRTUOUS WOMAN

Proverbs 31:19

During the time I initially penned this Bible study on the virtuous woman, we were without water and had been since early the day before. We had to do some excavating on our land and our water line was accidentally broken. After several unsuccessful attempts to repair the pipes, my husband and a few men from church had to call it quits around 10:30 that night, in hopes that sometime the next day we could have water. My husband was discouraged. However, I realized something in the light of all this trouble as I was pondering the next verse in our study of the virtuous woman, that being verse 19....

"She layeth her hands to the spindle, and her hands hold the distaff."

A spindle was a slender stick, which was twirled to twist drawn out fibers caught in a hook, or slot, at the top. A spindle whorl acted as a flywheel for more efficient twisting. Spun thread was wound onto the stick. Sometimes it was plied or twined, two or three threads being twisted together. The finished product could then be used for weaving. The distaff was a stick that held the fibers from which the thread was spun. In spinning, the virtuous woman would take the spindle in her right hand, by twisting which she twists the thread; while she holds the distaff, on which the wool or flax is rolled, in the guard of her left arm, and draws down the thread with the fingers of her left hand. Though difficult to explain, it is a very unique process, nonetheless.

In Exodus 35:25 it says, "And all the women that were wise hearted did spin with their hands, and brought that which they had spun, both of blue, and of purple, and of scarlet, and of fine linen."

As I related this to my personal situation in being without water, I realized that with every trial, I have the opportunity to take the good, as well as the bad fibers of life and guide them into a strong and useful thread for a future purpose! Here I was, faced with the choice to react miserably to not having water, or to react positively as that fiber was chosen by God to come into our home and all our lives that day. By His grace, I chose to react properly to a trying situation and in so doing it strengthened and encouraged my husband! He was greatly relieved that I was not distressed (as most husbands are!), and the fiber, or trial, became a <u>useful</u> thread woven into our lives. Noting the improvement in my husband's demeanor, immediately I thought back on all the times that I *did not* react properly when I could and should have! Perhaps you too, have those memories....

You see, ladies, the distaff, being the stick that held the fibers, represents the hand of the Lord. As we understand this process of spinning, one can't help but wonder how many fibers the Lord has sent into our lives to be intertwined with others. When we resist God's design for our lives, we create gaps in the very fabric that He is trying to create as we disregard His purposes… What good is fabric full of holes? Have we always reacted properly, thereby turning each circumstance into a useful thread woven into our own lives and those of our family members? How compliant are you, dear lady? The virtuous woman's hand is said as holding the distaff; therefore, she is working WITH the hand of the Lord. Are we truly laborers together with God today? Are we working with Him or against Him in our lives?

Acts 7:51a, "Ye stiffnecked and uncircumcised in heart and ears, ye do always resist the Holy Ghost..."

What happens to you when the Lord sends fibers your way with which to spin the threads of your life that you do not like? Do you faithfully spin those fibers anyway, accept them and twist them together with those you do like, guiding them both into a stronger thread, allowing God to create a greater purpose in your life through compliance to His pattern? Are trials simply sent to aggravate us, do we only "tolerate" them, or do we really believe Romans 8:28, "And we know that all things work together for good to them that love God, to them who are the called according to His purpose." The wise hearted woman will spin skillfully and wisely, the fibers that God chooses for her to spin with, bringing forth a strong thread that God can use to weave a wonderful work in and through her. One day we will bring to Him that which we have spun and lay it at His feet. What will your work look like - a tangled mess, a creation full of holes, a flimsy remnant, or a tightly woven and useful fabric? How closely will your life reflect the pattern God designed it to be?

Verse 26 of Exodus 35 goes on to say, "And all the women whose heart stirred them up in wisdom spun goats' hair."

Goats were used as a sacrifice before their hair was spun with, and ladies, we are going to need a *sacrificial* attitude while spinning the fibers sent us from the hand of God! Not everything that comes into our lives will be particularly enjoyable… We must lay aside our will, accept each discomfiting circumstance, and blend it gracefully and skillfully into the whole of our lives. Difficulties are not to be tossed on the scrap pile – there is great value in them! The virtuous woman was noted for her wisdom and her life of sacrifice, was she not? Both of these qualities were strong threads with which she spun. Are you spinning with these sturdy threads as well? Ladies, your work will not hold up without either quality, nor will God's plan for your life take shape apart from yielding to the hand of the Lord....

Romans 12:1, "I beseech you therefore, brethren, by the mercies of God, that ye present your bodies a living <u>sacrifice</u>, holy, acceptable unto God, which is your reasonable service."

Today I want to encourage you to seek the Lord for wisdom as you lay your hands to the spindle of your life... Are you weaving a strong home, a strong marriage, a strong walk with the Lord? Are you mad at God for the fibers He has chosen for you to spin with? Have you let go of the distaff and walked away from your responsibilities? What are your thoughts while your hands are busy spinning, as your fingers accept and guide each fiber sent by God – bitter or joyful? Are you impatient for a peek at His pattern?

Ladies, it takes a *lifetime* to weave virtuous qualities into us as women of God. Be patient. Be <u>compliant</u>. Let us accept each fiber with faith in the Lord and work together with Him! Oh, the difference we can make in our homes through every trial, and in every unpleasant situation that comes our way! Let us not whine in weakness but in wise heartedness and wisdom spin cheerfully....

Spin cheerfully,
Not tearfully,
Though wearily you plod;
Spin carefully,
Spin prayerfully,
But leave the thread with God.
The shuttles of His purpose move
To carry out His own design.
Seek not too soon to disapprove
His work, nor yet assign
Dark motives, when, with silent dread,
You view each somber fold;

For, lo! within each darker thread
There twines a thread of gold.
Spin cheerfully,
Not tearfully,
He knows the way you plod;
Spin carefully,
Spin prayerfully,
But leave the thread with God.

THE EXTENSION OF THE VIRTUOUS WOMAN

Proverbs 31:20

Do any of you exercise daily? Some of us wouldn't miss our chance to stay physically toned for anything! There is nothing like a good workout and a little stretching of our limbs, amen? Let us join the virtuous woman in verse 20, as she does her stretches....

"She stretcheth out her hand to the poor; yea, she reacheth forth her hands to the needy."

Is this the kind of workout you are regularly engaging in, dear lady? Could this inscription be engraved on your headstone after you have gone to be with the Lord, having left this world and opportunity behind? For the virtuous woman, this epitaph stands true, and her challenging inscription lies etched within Proverbs chapter 31 to remind us all of her widespread ministry - one that even reaches the heart of her Savior!

Proverbs 19:17a, "He that hath pity upon the poor lendeth unto the Lord…

How does the virtuous woman come to the place in her life where she has such a helpful attitude, such a ministry mindset toward others? What brings about her burden for the poor and needy? I daresay that it is her humility, for she has first seen *herself* as poor and needy….

Psalm 40:17 says, "But I am poor and needy; yet the Lord thinketh upon me: thou art my help and my deliverer; make no tarrying, O my Lord."

Because a woman of virtue *first* has a proper perspective of herself, there is no room for pride in her heart. Proverbs 31:20 describes the virtuous woman as one who stretches OUT and reaches FORTH. In other words, she goes above and beyond her normal activity to help others. She greatly extends herself… Likewise, we too can do the same as we place others before ourselves and choose to come <u>behind</u> people in service and support. You see, ladies, the virtuous woman does not think of herself as better than others or one who should be served, but takes upon the form of a servant, as Christ did.

Philip. 2:7, "But made himself of no reputation, and took upon him the form of a servant, and was made in the likeness of men:"

As women, we are always worrying about our form, or rather, our figures, aren't we? This concern is what drives us to be so faithful in our daily exercises! How about our spiritual figure?? Are you equally concerned? As the virtuous woman extends herself, her form becomes that of a *servant*! This is the result of her spiritual workout, the perfect shape her character takes on, and it is fit in the eyes of the Lord! Have you ever considered giving your spirit exercise, dear lady? We need the spiritual activity of <u>stretching forth</u> and <u>reaching out</u> to others, otherwise our **hearts** will get flabby! Instead of modeling ourselves after a Barbie doll, we should model ourselves after Jesus Christ...

Romans 8:32, "He that spared not his own Son, but delivered him up for us all, how shall he not with him also freely give us all things?"

The virtuous woman realizes that without Christ, she is - and was - poor and needy. Did the Lord tarry when He saw our needs? Certainly not! He thought on us, He placed value upon us; He gave His *life* for us! Ladies, our loving heavenly Father met each and every one of our needs at Calvary - the physical, emotional, and spiritual - and the virtuous woman is eternally grateful to her Lord for that! He stretched out His arms of love; He reached down from heaven and rescued us from hell – *sparing nothing*. It is out of gratefulness to her God that a woman of virtue extends herself to others that they might know the character of her Lord. She puts forth the same effort that Christ did...

Isaiah 25:4, "For thou hast been a strength to the poor, a strength to the needy in his distress, a refuge from the storm, a shadow from the heat, when the blast of the terrible ones is as a storm against the wall."

Ladies, do we see ourselves as poor and needy apart from the presence of God in our lives, or has self-sufficiency tainted our vision and hindered our outreach to others? How far are you willing to go to minister to people? How much are you willing to sacrifice?

2 Corinthians 8:9, "For ye know the grace of our Lord Jesus Christ, that, though he was rich, yet for your sakes he became poor, that ye through his poverty might be rich."

Have you ever found yourself highly selective concerning those you will stretch out your hand to? Have you been put off by the appearance or behavior of an individual and decided against reaching out to them because of their external form? Have you ever been guilty of only ministering to those who are nicest to you, or those you are the most confident or comfortable with, those you are certain approve of you? God's patience toward sinners is unbelievable – how about yours, dear lady??

Romans 10:21, "But to Israel he saith, All day long I have stretched out my hands unto a disobedient and gainsaying people."

When it comes to extending yourself, who would you invite to your house for dinner, or better yet, who WOULDN'T you invite and why? In Proverbs 25:21, the Bible exhorts us to give bread and water to even our enemies - not just our good friends! Yes, the virtuous woman extends herself because of who GOD is - not because of who man is! Are you a Christian woman who is spending less than what is honorable for the sake of her Lord? Have you been letting others determine the kind of Christian you are going to be, or is God the determining factor in your extension?

In Mark 12: 30& 31 the Bible says, "And thou shalt love the Lord thy God with all thy heart, and with all thy soul, and with all thy mind, and with all thy strength: this is the first commandment. And the second is like, namely this, Thou shalt love thy neighbor as thyself. There is none other commandment greater than these."

The word neighbor is defined as "a fellow being". That means your neighbor is just like *you*, just as poor and needy as *you* were without Christ!

 Your "neighbor" is the person who is near to you - the next person you meet. A virtuous woman must not choose her neighbor; she must take the neighbor that God sends her! She must reach out to that particular individual in love the same way Christ reached out to her.... Ladies, this love of our "neighbor" is the only door out of the dungeon of self!! It is the only way to take on the form of a servant....

Proverbs 3:28, "Say not unto thy neighbor, Go, and come again, and tomorrow I will give; when thou hast it by thee."

Because the virtuous woman has manages well her time, talents and money, she has her home in order and can effectively reach out to others. By the way, to extend yourself does not mean you abandon your family to do so; it is *included* in the management of your time! A woman of virtue stretches her budget, her time, her attention, and yes, her *patience*, so that it covers an immeasurable area of ministry. She is sensitive to all those in need, spots them quickly, and is quick to help, having made sure that she has the resources available, both spiritually and physically, to do so. She has a great God who will supply her every need as well as theirs - and seeks to prove it!

Proverbs 22:9, "He that hath a bountiful eye shall be blessed; for he giveth of his bread to the poor."

2 Corinthians 9:6, "But this I say, He which soweth sparingly shall reap also sparingly; and he which soweth bountifully shall reap also bountifully."

Because she stretches forth and reaches out to others, the virtuous woman's heart is in great shape, and joy becomes part of her character!

She is a happy woman knowing that she has been instrumental in making a difference in the lives of others. She wastes not any opportunity, knowing it would be a transgression to pass up what God would have her to do.

Proverbs 14:21, "He that despiseth his neighbor sinneth: but he that hath mercy on the poor, happy is he."

In closing, let us each be willing to reach out to *anyone* on God's behalf. If you have a parsimonious disposition, that is, a disposition to save expense, your heart needs the exercise! It's time we broadened our personal outreach. Remember that God spared nothing in reaching out to you… *Extend* yourself. Get your spiritual workout in everyday!

The bread that bringeth strength I want to give;
The water pure that bids the thirsty live.
I want to help the fainting, day by day.
I'm sure I shall not pass again this way.

I want to give the oil of joy for tears,
The faith to conquer crowding doubts and fears,
Beauty for ashes may I give alway.
I'm sure I shall not pass again this way.

I want to give good measure running o'er,
And into angry hearts I want to pour
The answer soft that turneth wrath away.
I'm sure I shall not pass again this way.

I want to give to others hope and faith;
I want to do all that the Master saith;
I want to do aright from day to day.
I'm sure I shall not pass again this way.

THE REGULARITY OF THE VIRTUOUS WOMAN

Proverbs 31:21

~ Behind Time ~

The best laid plans, the most important affairs, and the fortunes of individuals, the wealth of nations, honor, life itself, are daily sacrificed because somebody is *"behind time."*

There are men who always fail in whatever they undertake simply because they are *"behind time."*

There are others who put off reformation year by year, till death seizes them; and they perish unrepentant, because they are for ever *"behind time."*

Five minutes in a crisis is worth years. It is but a little period, yet it has often saved a fortune or redeemed a people.

If there is one virtue that should be cultivated more than another by him who would succeed in life, it is punctuality; if there is one error that should be avoided, it is being *"behind time."*

Proverbs 31:21

"She is not afraid of the snow for her household: for all her household are clothed with scarlet."

This is our verse today, ladies, and in essence, we observe that the virtuous woman is not "*behind time*". She knows tough times will come but purposes in her heart not to be overtaken by them and is rarely caught off-guard. She is personally prepared for any change that might arrive and has her household prepared for those changes as well! Each member is primed for the various storms of life; those cold winds that threaten to blow annually, even the rains and floods that may come in the spring. A woman of virtue can accept the blowing of those winds confidently, and all her household is clothed with scarlet and sheltered from the sting and effects yearly storms can bring....

Matthew 7:25, "And the rain descended, and the floods came, and the winds blew, and beat upon that house; and it fell not: for it was founded upon a rock."

So it is with the storms of life, ladies.... Spiritually speaking, per annum we will encounter "cold winds" which blow upon our homes, won't we? What will your reaction be? How will your family hold up? The regularity of your life is a strong determining factor! Do you typically scramble to prepare for storms at the last minute? Do you find that you and your family suffer for your irregularity, your lack of routine preparation? At times those cold winds contain an accompanying snowfall that can quickly accumulate to surprising depth, lingering for weeks before melting, crippling all progress....

With strong spring storms, torrential rains drop down and floodwaters rise to totally wipe out everything, leaving nothing behind but a path of destruction. Will you be able to withstand seasonal changes in temperature or the conditions of life during such trying times? Think about it... Is your household truly set for anything, or are you *"behind time"* in preparing for them?

The scarlet spoken of in verse 21 that the virtuous woman's household is clothed with, we can liken to being in Christ. He is the rock we must be founded upon. When we are in Christ and ordering our lives by His Word, you and I will naturally be prepared for *any* storm that might come our way. *The steadiness of our devotions brings steadiness to our lives.* We will be able to endure the snow for however long it lingers – even the unexpected blizzards - because of the strength and stability the Lord will provide us! The virtuous woman does well to see to it that each member of her home knows the Lord Jesus Christ as their personal Savior and is clothed with scarlet, that precious blood of the Lamb! Is everyone at your house born-again, dear lady? Are they properly prepared for the future, for *eternity*? Why fear for them - make sure! Nothing brings a mother more peace of mind than to know her children are clothed in scarlet....

3 John 1:4, "I have no greater joy than to hear that my children walk in truth."

A woman of virtue understands that her little ones will also be faced with the same storms that she has encountered year after year in her lifetime. When her days on earth are ended, she can close her eyes and pass into eternity in peace knowing that her household was adequately prepared for life's storms from the Word of God as she taught and lived it before them. "She is not afraid of snow..."

No worries, no fears; the unknown is not a scary monster that looms on the horizon. Sound good to you?? You see, ladies, the virtuous woman spends her entire life seeing to it that her household will survive long after she is gone. With regularity she instills in her children strength of character rooted in Christ; rich, godly character that is prepared to handle life victoriously! In properly preparing our children to survive in this world, we will not have as many worries or fears when they leave the nest. We will be confident in their relationship with Jesus Christ and His leadership in their lives! Don't wait until the last year they are home to finally equip them... Are you teaching your children how to properly lean on the LORD, or are they tied to YOU in such a way that when you died they would die too? Would that be the great flood that would wash them away, or would they be able to go on? Ladies, if their only walk is with **you,** they won't survive, for you are not the rock they should be founded upon! However, if their walk is with **God**, they will make it!

Proverbs 22:3 says, "A prudent man forseeth the evil and hideth himself: but the simple pass on and is punished."

How do you feel about that snow spoken of in Proverbs 31:21 today? Are you afraid your family wouldn't hold up under the weight of it? Have you taken the time to anticipate the sin that lies ahead of those precious ones you are responsible for and faithfully prepared them to be over comers, or are there areas you are behind in training them in? Are you prepared yourself?? Have you buried yourself regularly in the Word of God and the wisdom it provides, or are you behind in your Bible reading? Do you know what melts snow? SALT!

The Word of God is salt; it is a preservative... No matter how much snow a storm may bring your way, God's Word can preserve you from its effects and melt away the burdens of life! What wisdom are you going to pass along to your children if your speech is not seasoned with salt from God's Word??

What good is your presence in their vulnerable lives if you are not going to heartily prepare them for the future? Govern their lives by *steady* practice of truth. Give them some salt *now* so they can throw it on their snow later....

Col. 4:6, "Let your speech be alway with grace, seasoned with salt, that ye may know how ye ought to answer every man."

Matthew 5:13, "Ye are the salt of the earth: but if the salt have lost his savour, wherewith shall it be salted? it is thenceforth good for nothing, but to be cast out, and to be trodden under foot of men."

Maybe you have convinced yourself that "bad weather" will never come your way - it has been so comfortable and warm where you live, surely a storm would never hit there! The Bible says the simple pass on and are punished - you'll end up destroyed by such ridiculous, fly-by-night thinking.... Wouldn't you rather face life in confidence and face that evil day head on, free from fear...." and having done all, to stand" as Ephesians 6:13 describes?

Yes, salt keeps you from slipping and sliding in the snowy times and helps you to stand confidently! In Nahum 2:3, scripture mentions that the valiant men are clothed in scarlet. I want to see each member of my household <u>valiant</u>, how about you? Are they so?? Faint-hearted, timid behavior results from a deficiency in uniform order, from proper methodical scriptural training. Is anyone in your home *"behind time"*? Just as you systematically dig out those warmer clothes to protect you and your family from cold winter winds and storms that blow through this time of year, be sure that you are also systematically digging out truth for those spiritual storms and cold days ahead!

Make sure everyone is wearing scarlet and don't forget to spread some SALT around your house too. We can't afford to squander the present so stay on track. Those who kill time will soon find that time kills them! Because of her regularity in maintaining a steady course, a woman of virtue is never "behind time".... nor is anyone in her household.

THE ATTIRE OF THE VIRTUOUS WOMAN

Proverbs 31:22

"She maketh herself coverings of tapestry; her clothing is silk and purple."

I don't know about you but I became convicted on the second word of this verse! "She *maketh*...." With all the other things we have witnessed so far that the virtuous woman accomplishes, she even finds time to sew! We learned in verse 21 that her household was clothed with scarlet, representative of an attractively colored high quality fabric also used for the curtains of the Tabernacle. Naturally, her household would stand out as well dressed. As I said before, I believe that every verse listed in this chapter is listed in the order of the virtuous woman's priorities. If you remember the scriptures we've covered so far, her husband's heart was mentioned first, and then her home, and then we got a glimpse of what she performed outside of her home. As we continue to observe the various details of her life, a woman of virtue is found taking care of the wardrobe needs of her family first, and then lastly her own...

Philip. 2:4, "Look not every man on his own things, but every man also on the things of others."

Let me take a moment to say a little something on the side here. Have you ever been somewhere and noticed a woman all decked out in nice clothing while her children by her look like homeless street urchins with what they were wearing? I have! It surely gives the woman the appearance of self-centeredness, amen? One is not inclined to think such a mother is in the habit of putting her children ahead of herself... On one occasion, as my children and I were out doing some grocery shopping, an older gentleman approached us and said, "Excuse me, my wife and I were just noticing what a nice looking family you have. You are all clean and nicely dressed and you carry yourselves well, it is refreshing to see!" I don't mind telling you that compliment greatly encouraged me! The appearance of the children is always a reflection on the woman of the home, for she is usually the overseer who dresses the household.

Proverbs 29:15, ".... a child left to himself bringeth his mother to shame."

Mom, do you leave it up to your kids to choose what they will wear or do you wisely supervise their choices – even in the stores? You will have fewer arguments over their clothing selections if you pay attention to the BUYING of sensible clothes to begin with! Do your children pass your eyes of inspection before going out in public? We have "around the house" clothes, and we have "going out" clothes. Nobody leaves the house with dirty faces or messy hair, no clothing is to be revealing, no shirts untucked, no worldly slogans, no clothes with holes, no muddy shoes, etc. (I absolutely *despise* those baggy, saggy, raggy pants!) Before we enter a public place, I always remind my children WHO they are representing - the Lord Jesus Christ! It is up to their mother to train them properly in this area of dress, and my example ought to match my motto. By the way, how do YOU look when go out, dear mother? Even though the virtuous woman took care of herself last – she doesn't have to look like she did!

I was reminded the day we were complimented of just how closely people watch others. After they inspect the parents, they inspect the children - the whole family paints a portrait of the home! Don't ever think that people don't notice your family as a *whole*… As a Christian, and a woman of virtue, you ought to care about the way you present yourselves to the general public.

2 Cor. 5:20a, "Now then we are ambassadors for Christ…"

All that having been said, let us get take a closer look at how the virtuous woman is dressed....

First, we see from our main verse that it was a priority of the virtuous woman to appear in public COVERED. Most times "fashion" limits this priority and personal desire for modesty. Certainly sewing something suitable takes care of such a problem. I think the need for this is rapidly growing... Each time I make a trip to the stores to find something modest for my daughter or I, we end up going home empty handed and disappointed. Sewing can be fun and makes nicer things affordable as well as ignites a spark of creativity in an eager seamstress. One can make something personally flattering to their size, shape and color. Consequently, a gratifying feeling of accomplishment results after the custom-made garment is finished and then proudly worn!

As we step into the closet of the virtuous woman and turn on the light, we find tapestry and silk and purple... But I thought that Christian women were expected to wear denim jumpers and white sneakers?! "How come the virtuous woman is able to own such an outstanding wardrobe?! I could never afford such attire!" Is that what you are thinking? Remember, the virtuous woman manages well the affairs of her household and is therefore able to purchase quality merchandise. There is no need for us to settle for a "frumpy" reputation!

I have heard it said that we wear 20% of our wardrobes 80% of the time. I would have to agree that much of our clothing hangs within our closets patiently waiting to be worn. Most of your shirts, if taken off the hangers, have permanent points in the shoulders from being suspended in one spot for so long, amen? Ladies, we *waste* what should be utilized more frequently. I challenge you to go to your closets today and try to remember the last time you wore each item. Perhaps there is there something you could trade in for silk and purple...

Proverbs 18:9, "He also that is slothful in his work is brother to him that is a great waster."

Did you notice that the virtuous woman does not rely on the revealing of her body parts for attractiveness? The *quality* of her coverings and the *color* of her coverings is made mention of. Tapestry is similar to embroidery, a very detailed and artistic work woven throughout with gold and silver. Ladies, are these the details people are overcome by when you enter a room, or is it that your dress is skin tight and low cut, revealing both cleavage and thigh? Beauty is abused if modesty does not accompany it! I know I have mentioned this before but we need to dress modestly as Christian women and exhort others to do so as well! Being a Christian woman doesn't mean we have to become known as thrift store advocates as our only alternative to fashion. Nor must we overreact and appear half dressed either! Pick fabrics, colors, and accessories that flatter, not flaunt. Purple was a color obtained from the secretion of a species of shellfish, which was found in the Mediterranean, particularly in the coasts of Phoenicia and Asia Minor. The coloring matter in each separate shellfish amounted to only a single drop; hence, the great value of this dye. Kings and high officers wore robes of this color. Purple was also worn by the wealthy and luxurious. With this color was associated the idea of royalty and majesty. While you may not feel like a queen today, if you are born-again, you have been adopted into the family of the King of King's! It's time we dressed accordingly...

1 Peter 2:9, "But ye are a chosen generation, a **royal** priesthood, an holy nation, a peculiar people; that ye should shew forth the praises of him who hath called you out of darkness into his marvellous light:"

Let us go back for a moment to verse 12 of Proverbs chapter 4 where the Bible talks about a virtuous woman as being a crown to her husband. Yes, he is the king of the home. We all understand a king wears a crown. Would a crown that embellishes a king be drab and colorless, minus the existence of vibrant, lively jewels, having no splendor at all to gaze upon? Of course not! A crown is suitably adorned for the king's head and the king's office, or rather his position. Let me ask you this question… With your husband residing as the king of your house, do you come across as his queen? On the other hand, do you "look like something the cat dragged in" as the old expression goes? Do you enhance his reputation by the way you dress or are you subtracting from it? What about the Lord's reputation in you?? To better illustrate my point, let's eavesdrop on King Ahasuerus and Queen Esther for a moment in Esther 5:1-2:

"Now it came to pass on the third day, that Esther put on her royal apparel, and stood in the inner court of the King's house, over against the King's house: and the King sat upon his royal throne in the royal house, over against the gate of the house. And it was so, when the king saw Esther the queen standing in the court, that she obtained favour in his sight...."

We find that when the queen was in the presence of the king her wardrobe was comprised of regal attire. She took pains to look nice when her husband was around. She enhanced his office with her person… Yes, she put away her sweat suit and old sneaks and donned her royal apparel *for him*. No doubt, this queen possessed a creative selection of garments she knew would be pleasurable to his eye. I don't have to tell you that men are visually attracted do I, ladies?? We would do well to remember that fact when dressing for the day, even at home during the week!

Most times, we only dress in our regal attire for church on Sundays... Put on some royal apparel and please your husband's eye! Why allow another woman to do that?? Obtain *favor* in his sight and spare him from having to see the same old thing on you! Dress in silk and purple and help him to forget the worldly women he may have seen all day! Give him something glorious to remember when he leaves for work and something glorious to look forward to come home to! He may say it doesn't matter, but just you watch and see....

Genesis 26:7-8, "And the men of the place asked him of his wife; and he said, She is my sister: for he feared to say, She is my wife; lest, said he, the men of the place should kill me for Rebekah; because she was fair to look upon. And it came to pass, when he had been there a long time, that Abimelech king of the Philistines looked out at a window, and saw, and, behold, Isaac was sporting with Rebekah his wife."

As I mentioned earlier, when you go out in public, dress appropriately so that you bring respect to your husband's position as king of your home. My children and I represent the home of Paul A. Iannello as well as the Lord Jesus Christ. Both reputations are to be taken into consideration, amen? Whose home do you and your children represent? How does your husband prefer to see you dressed? Is there anything he doesn't like to see you wear in public? Do you even care about the way you look? Consider whether your husband may be embarrassed about your appearance... If you don't know - humble yourself and ASK! He may say he doesn't care, but *you* still can, and he'll be grateful for the discretion he may lack that you exercise!

Do you ensure that your children change their play clothes for ones that look nicer before you go out in public so that your king's house appears in order, or do you never give it a thought? What about your family's testimony for the Lord?? A woman of virtue looks well to the ways of her household and makes sure that her husband has no need of spoil... An unkempt appearance to your family brings spoil upon the name of your husband and the Lord, ladies! Dress decently and do them both good and not evil, amen?

Yes, the virtuous woman's closet - the *queen's* closet - is filled with royal apparel that adequately covers her and compliments her king, acquiring favor in his sight. Not just her, but the whole household is dressed appropriately! Take complete inventory of your wardrobe today, won't you, dear lady? Give some thought to the details of your attire... Do you need to borrow some ideas from the virtuous woman or do you have silk and purple of your own to wear, and tapestry? In closing, I will leave you with this borrowed thought....

~A Slovenly Woman~

The most disgusting thing on earth is a slatternly woman. I mean, a woman who never combs her hair until she goes out, or looks like a fright until somebody calls. That a man married to one of these creatures stays at home as little as possible is no wonder! It is a wonder that such a man does not go on a whaling voyage of three years, and in a leaky ship. Costly wardrobe is not required; but, O woman, if you are not willing, by all that ingenuity of refinement can effect, to make yourself attractive to your husband, you ought not to complain if he seek in other society those pleasant surroundings which you deny him. — TALMAGE.

THE HUSBAND OF THE VIRTUOUS WOMAN

Proverbs 31:23

"Her husband is known in the gates, when he sitteth among the elders of the land."

Here is the positive influence a woman of virtue has on her husband's life. This too, is a consequence of all that she has accomplished, the fruit of her labors in his life. Just for a moment, let us reflect back on what this woman has been doing so far....

She seeketh, worketh, bringeth, riseth, giveth, considereth, planteth, girdeth, strengtheneth, perceiveth, layeth, stretcheth, reacheth, maketh...Whew! This gal has been burning up some calories!

What is her husband depicted as doing? "He sitteth....". I know from first hand experience that at times we feel this way about our husbands, don't we ladies? We tend to believe that we are taking care of most everything while our men enjoy a trouble-free existence. Buzzing around like little bees trying to get everything accomplished in 24 hours, we glance over at our husbands who, in our estimation, are only "sitting" around. At times, it might even be tempting to give in to a sour attitude... Yet, the virtuous woman strongly guards herself against bitterness!

Hebrews 12:14 & 15 says, "Follow peace with all men, and holiness, without which no man shall see the Lord: Looking diligently lest any man fail of the grace of God; lest any root of bitterness springing up trouble you, and thereby many be defiled."

Ladies, a woman of virtue keeps the garden of her heart free of weeds! No roots of bitterness are allowed to spring up and choke the good produce that is thriving in her life, and in her home. Women are quick to follow peace with everyone but their husbands. With them, it is *war*! The fruit of our labors at home should end in righteousness, not bitterness, anger and strife. A virtuous woman understands if even *one* weed takes root in her heart against her husband, scores of people will be ruined. In case you haven't noticed, your imagination feeds your thoughts and then your thoughts intensify your feelings… How do you feel about your husband these days?? What have you been dwelling on mentally?? Have you been practicing silent ridicule, microscopically concentrating on all his flaws until all reverence for him has been dissolved?? The husband of a virtuous woman is known in the gates as having the reputation of one whose wife *respects* him. Would that be your husband's reputation, dear lady?? You can quickly and easily spot contempt in a wife and immediately one's opinion of the man is formed. Certainly there is an air of power and authority that belongs to a highly respected man, one God can and will use in a mighty way! A well ordered home and a highly respected man is a perfect target of attack for the devil, and we need to seriously guard our homes - and our hearts - against bitterness toward our men. Much is at stake!

Ephes. 4:31, "Let all bitterness, and wrath, and anger, and clamour, and evil speaking, be put away from you, with all malice.."

These two individuals - the virtuous woman and her husband - are a team. He is known in the gates for his honorable reputation while she is known at home for her faithfulness. Having distinguished their God-given roles of responsibility, each is pleased to execute their duties with an earnest desire to honor God and serve others. The virtuous woman is not miffed that she is not the one acknowledged in the gates; she does not *compete* with her husband but *completes* him – his personal reputation and his ministry. Side by side, this team affects others for the cause of Christ and in turn store up for themselves treasures in heaven....

1 Cor. 9:17, "For if I do this thing willingly, I have a reward...."

Eccles. 4:9, "Two are better than one; because they have a good reward for their labour."

If you have ever studied this topic before, you might remember that the gates of the city, where the virtuous woman's husband is seated among the elders, is a place of high honor. Many important matters took place at these gates. Prophets and teachers brought their messages here, even the King held public audience at the gates. It was a place to meet new people and most of the men passed through the gate every day as they came and went with their business dealings. It was also the place where the city was protected and where the tower was located to spy out the enemy. So too, the town bums were found lying around. Rebellious children were brought to the gates by their parents to be stoned. Criminals were brought to be punished without the gates, and judgment for crimes was declared at the gates. What a mission field! Yes, this was definitely a place where a well-respected man was needed and where the virtuous woman's husband was found.

His opinion was highly valued because his home was in order.... If only we had more godly men in the gates of the cities of America! If only we had more godly homes behind those gates, homes with godly women dwelling within them, women who are delighted to be there.... A city is only as strong as the homes within it, as is the nation! Let us fill our country back up with strength and righteousness...

Proverbs 29:2, "When the righteous are in authority, the people rejoice: but when the wicked beareth rule, the people mourn."

Lament. 1:20, "Behold, O Lord; for I am in distress: my bowels are troubled; mine heart is turned within me; for I have grievously rebelled: abroad the sword bereaveth, at home there is as death.

Yes, the virtuous woman was proud to have her husband seated in such a place of honor and it was because of her support that he confidently carried out this vocation in an effective manner. I want to stop here for just a moment and exhort you ladies to be sure that you are edifying your husband in a way that helps him to better perform his various responsibilities. Do not be so foolish as to pluck him apart with your criticisms! The Bible says that the wise woman *builds* her house! Send him out strengthened to do God's work, wherever that might be for your husband today. Realize the enemy will be there to try to weaken him, so do not add to his troubles and make the devil's job easier with your uprisings! Work together <u>with God</u> for the good of your husband, for the good of your home, for the good of the land! Today the sword of the Lord is missing from the land and Christian homes are dying out! Be instrumental in keeping righteousness alive, don't be bitter that your husband is gone to handle the affairs of the city - be about your own business with joy and purpose.

1 Kings 5:5, "And, behold, I purpose to build an house unto the name of the Lord my God...."

I'm sure that the virtuous woman's husband both saw and listened to grieving subject matter day after day at the gates. Perhaps he had to be one of those that threw the stones at a rebellious child.... Certainly, his heart grew heavy and his body grew weary with the weight of the various issues he had to deal with daily. Maybe he joined in with the preaching and tried to minister to those homeless people scattered here and there. Political discussions can be tense, and I'm sure that this man had his share of controversial conversations everyday. Men are not as thrilled about talking as frequently as women are, and yet the gates of the city is where much vital communication took place; he must've had to talk all day long! No doubt, he probably wasn't much of a conversationalist when the business day was ended. Yet, perhaps there was still a spring to his step as he made his way home! *Home*, where he knew he had a wonderful woman waiting for him who would look and smell nice when he arrived, who had dinner ready and things in order. All day long the virtuous woman was busy filling the atmosphere of her husband's home with love and strength – the two qualities that equipped him to turn around and fulfill his God-given responsibilities in the gates again the next day. Yes, his heart safely trusted in her, even when it seemed that the world around him was worsening! He knew his wife would remain steadfast and faithful to him - and to her God. They were a team and he considered himself a very blessed man and thanked God for such a woman - a virtuous woman whose price was far above rubies!

Proverbs 3:15, "She is more precious than rubies: and all the things thou canst desire are not to be compared unto her."

What a picture this couple paints for us today... The virtuous woman was working behind the scenes and her husband was working out in front while God was glorified in them both. The Lord was pleased with a couple that He could count on to minister in the city He had placed them... They respected one another and others respected both of them. It was a well ordered home and one that the Lord could and often did use to draw others to Him. I hope you have been challenged today, as I have, to strive to have such a positive influence in your husband's life, your home, your city, and ultimately for the cause of Christ!

THE EARNINGS OF THE VIRTUOUS WOMAN

Proverbs 31:24

"She maketh fine linen and selleth it; and delivereth girdles unto the merchant."

We perceive that the virtuous woman, in the wise management of her time, also has a small home business on the side. She *maketh* and *delivereth* that which she already has the equipment and supplies for at home. In verse 13, the Bible shows that she has already purchased the linen supplies, and in verse 19, we find the virtuous woman lays her hand to the spindle she owns. While she is busy putting her needle to good work, in addition to her own private creations, further quantity is produced for profit. Ladies, that means she carries out this extra work - *at home*! After it was completed and a reasonable measure wrought, her designs were then delivered to the merchants to sell. A woman of virtue applies herself to the business proper for a woman to conduct... She didn't pursue schooling to become a busy executive in a corporation having to work demanding hours, or try her wings at construction work alongside the men of the world; she simply used the same talents that prospered her home to bring in extra money. What were her boundaries for this extra work? Let us go back to verse 10 of this study in Proverbs 31, where we recall that her deepest concerns are with her husband's heart. He is her first priority! In reviewing verses 13-22, the responsibilities a woman of virtue carries out from day to day are listed - in order of importance. Then as we skim down to verse 23, her husband is once more mentioned for holding a position of high regard in the community. You can't ignore the fact that only with these important matters properly attended to is the virtuous woman then referred to as making and selling fine linens and girdles. Her choice of what she will do with her spare time is based on that which GOD regards as most important....

Matthew 6:33, "But seek ye first the kingdom of God, and his righteousness; and all these things shall be added unto you."

Ladies, you must guard your relationship with the Lord in every profitable venture you consider! Affirm that your time with God will not suffer loss, for the rest of your family falls within the boundaries of your heart. If your heart suffers, so will they... The limits of a virtuous woman are set by the priorities of her home and they being met **first**. The husband of the virtuous woman had no problem with the implementing of her skills for profit, for his heart safely trusted in her judgments and management of her time. He knows that she will never permit anything to rise above her home. One can gather from this study, that the extra work mentioned was accomplished *when she had the time*, not when the merchants demanded it be done!! The virtuous woman does not place herself in a position where the world dictates the use of her time; *she* maintains full control and management of it. At what time the items to be sold for profit were completed, were they delivered; a very simple plan with no pressure on anyone! A virtuous woman allows nothing to steal from her home, for her heart is set upon it. Her primary source of livelihood was found within those four walls; her self-worth, and her *joy*. What outside work could ever replace or compare to such a high calling as the one she already had?

1 Tim. 5:14, "I will therefore that the younger women marry, bear children, guide the house, give none occasion to the adversary to speak reproachfully."

Perhaps you have been wrestling with the decision of bringing in a little extra money. Be careful and prayerful in making this decision! First, consider your relationship with the Lord. Is it as strong as it should be, or once was? Are you faithful in your daily devotions; is your record of accomplishment such that nothing hinders your time with the Lord? Have you developed that daily discipline yet?

Next, your husband's heart should be consulted; he should be at total peace with this decision, for he is the king of your home and the first one who will stand to suffer if all goes awry! Will he be taking a back seat to the extra work you wish to take on? Will your relationship suffer in any way for taking on the added responsibility? If this is the case, abandon all thought of the extra load. Your home is your first responsibility, dear lady, and one that you would do well to be faithful with! Will the work you are considering remove your presence from your home? Think next of the children God has given you… Will your children suffer in any way in this decision? Will they have to be placed in the care of someone else besides their mother for you to carry out the labor? Will someone else be dictating to you when you will deliver your efforts or will you remain in full control of your time? While shopping in Wal-mart recently, I overheard a conversation between two older female employees who had been scheduled to work through the holidays. They were discussing how upsetting it was for them to be unable to be home to prepare dinner or gather with their families on these special occasions. They had no say in the use of their time....

Psalm 90:12, "So teach us to number our days, that we may apply our hearts unto wisdom."

Jeremiah 10:12, "He hath made the earth by his power, <u>he hath established the world by his wisdom</u>, **and hath stretched out the heavens by his discretion**."

Extend yourself wisely – God did! Don't leave off discretion when you are looking to enlarge your involvement in other worlds outside of your home. The Bible exhorts us not to waste our precious lives in vain pursuits… Is the additional burden really worth it?? How will your attitude be affected? How about the outlook of your family members?

Will you become weary, worn and lacking in patience over the added pressure, causing your family to receive your leftovers and not your firstfruits? Will you be short with them; will your voice level increase in volume by way of all you have to accomplish on a daily basis? No doubt your loved ones will suffer in your absence, sense your pressures, and become frustrated themselves. Let us keep our priorities in order and spare the aggravation upon our homes! Are you keeping your house or losing it in your quest for financial gain?? Divide your time up wisely....

Mark 3:25, "And if a house be divided against itself, that house cannot stand."

Maybe you have already placed yourself in this position and have realized that you have lost sight of your home and the importance of it. Things are in total disarray… You have allowed the pursuit of extra money bring you into bondage and discovered such riches lack pleasantness to them. Your walk with God is bankrupt, your marriage has undergone great strain, your children have suffered, and you are frazzled and worn… Now what?? It is simple - get out of it! Get back *home* and get control of your spirit, your marriage, your children, and your priorities in general. Home is the place where your livelihood is rooted, where the secret to peace and contentment lies. If the virtuous woman has gone astray from her home, it only stands to reason that the virtuous qualities that once inhabited the chambers of her house will also be missing…

Haggai 2:3, "Who is left among you that saw this house in her first glory? and how do ye see it now?...."

Matthew 23:38, "Behold, your house is left unto you desolate."

If you can utilize the talents that prosper your home and perform extra work within the boundaries set up for us in the Word of God, then amen. It can only be accomplished when done in an orderly way. There are many thriving home businesses where all family members are involved. However, please do not lose sight of what is most important - keep your priorities in order and maintain control of your time! Make your decisions wisely, and remember to guard that orderly home that the devil so likes to attack and destroy!

Proverbs 24:3-4, "Through wisdom is an house builded; and by understanding it is established: And by knowledge shall the chambers be filled with all precious and pleasant riches."

THE STYLE OF THE VIRTUOUS WOMAN

Proverbs 31:25

"Strength and honour are her clothing; and she shall rejoice in time to come."

As we opened the closet of the virtuous woman, we discovered that it was filled with tapestry, silk and purple. When putting together her "outfit" for the day, these quality materials were chosen from. What about her "infit"? Though she looks very nicely put together outwardly, the beauty within a woman of virtue is what shines brightest when others are in her presence. This is a beauty that cannot be hidden, a style all her own that cannot be overlooked. Coupled with her lovely appearance, she was prepared *inwardly* for any occasion....

Psalm 45:13 says, "The King's daughter is all glorious within: her clothing is of wrought gold."

Ladies, while we take great pains to look attractive externally, we must also consider the condition of our inward character, and how our *insides* are doing. Is it all glorious within you today? Are you dressed and prepared to handle life on the *inside* of yourself? What is your style?? You see ladies, as a virtuous woman's heart and life are tested and tried, scripture teaches that a daughter of the King comes forth as gold, for strength and honor are part of her inward wardrobe. She is found a vessel unto praise and honour in God's eyes....

1 Peter 1:7, "That the trial of your faith, being much more precious than of gold that perisheth, though it be tried with fire, might be found unto praise and honour and glory at the appearing of Jesus Christ."

Zechariah 13:9, "And I will bring the third part through the fire, and will refine them as silver is refined, and will try them as gold is tried: they shall call on my name, and I will hear them: I will say, It is my people: and they shall say, The Lord is my God."

Ladies, be sure you are not inwardly dressed in fashion that is flammable, a character style that is set ablaze under the pressures and trials that come upon us all from day to day. We wouldn't dream of wearing outward clothing that would easily ignite, would we? Neither should our character be found clad in such hazardous garments! God says He will bring us through the fire to refine us, to prove to us what the condition of our character is; what will happen to you when that day comes? Will God's strength be found **in** you, or will your character disintegrate under the heat?

Romans 5:6 says that, "For when we were yet without strength, in due time Christ died for the ungodly."

There was a time when the virtuous woman, as was the case with you and I, was without strength, when we were lost in our trespasses and sins. However, Christ died for us and provided us with the opportunity to have His strength existing within us as a part of our spiritual adornment through the indwelling presence of the Holy Spirit. That inner strength comes at salvation but grows with time and testing. A woman of virtue has put on the Lord Jesus Christ through salvation in Him, continuing to add to her strength in her daily choices as a Christian. She sports a *new* style of behavior…

Romans 13:14, "But put ye on the Lord Jesus Christ and make no provision for the flesh to fulfill the lusts thereof."

It is no secret that the choices we make turn around and make us. To put it simply, strength comes from making proper choices in our lives. What have your choices been lately? Have you become a stronger Christian through them, or have they left you weaker spiritually, stripped of inward beauty?

The Bible says to make no provision for your flesh; don't choose unrighteousness as your style! We are to make *holy* choices that lead toward greater strength in God....

Ephes. 4:24, "And that ye put on the new man, which after God is created in righteousness and true holiness."

1 Timothy 2: 9 & 10, "In like manner also, that women adorn themselves in modest apparel, with shamefacednes and sobriety; not with broided hair, or gold, or pearls, or costly array; But (which becometh women professing godliness) with good works."

Today there are many Christian women who profess godliness - yet do not possess godliness *inwardly*, they are naked in godly character. The choices they are making on a daily basis are not matching up with their words. Their selfish conduct is not leading them toward beauty of character, for they are not yielding to the Holy Spirit that dwells within them! Ladies, the fear of the Lord is the beauty of the soul! What are you wearing inwardly? Godliness is put on through the choices you make, and with them comes His strength. Do you think God is going to add muscle to your moral fiber when you are choosing your own way rather than His? How are you holding up under the storms of life these days? Do the least little things set you off, find you flaring up under pressure?

Proverbs 24:10, "If thou faint in the day of adversity, thy strength is small."

Ladies, the virtuous woman has endurance, the firmness necessary to bear up under pressure, trials, and disappointments in life. She has properly dressed herself inwardly; there is not an area of her heart where God's strength is not abiding! She wears His strength everywhere she goes and is never caught dressed without it. As one of the Kings' daughters, to be without your heavenly Father's strength is to be naked in character! Physically speaking, public nudity is termed "indecent exposure." Spiritually speaking, it is equally indecent when we let "self" hang out all over the place. Women of virtue must be properly dressed inwardly…

Job 29:14, "I put on righteousness, and it clothed me…."

It is a goal of the virtuous woman that her life would be a clear testimony of strength rooted in the Lord. It becomes a crown of glory to her in her old age… During her lifetime, she desires to pass God's strength along to others. His strength has a long lasting effect on those she has helped and ministered to over time. Are you extending God's strength of character toward your children, dear mother? Do we care that others see, have seen, and continue to see this strength in us?? Are others desirous of copying the style of your spirit? Is inner strength something that you think happens by accident, or an inner wardrobe donned intentionally? How many women do you think would be very excited to learn that an entire wardrobe of beautiful dresses had been purchased for them? We all love to look attractive outwardly… However, consider today your inward beauty. With the blood of His Son, our heavenly Father has purchased a spectacular inner wardrobe for us to dress ourselves with! All we have to do is put it on… I hope you have learned today that strength can only be worn as you yield to the Lord in your life. Are you wearing it today??

Psalm 71:18, "Now also when I am old and grayheaded, O God, forsake me not; until I have shewed thy strength unto this generation, and thy power to every one that is to come."

Now that we have added strength to our inward wardrobes, let us consider honor – another characteristic that is part of the inward beauty of the virtuous woman...

Proverbs 15:33, "The fear of the Lord is the instruction of wisdom; and before honour is humility."

We have seen the humility of the virtuous woman as she chooses to live the life of a servant, joyfully meeting the many needs of others. This too, is a choice.... She has chosen humility and daily adorns herself with this attribute inwardly; it is a style inseparable from her strength!

Proverbs 29:23 says, "A man's pride shall bring him low: but honour shall uphold the humble in spirit."

Humility brings a gentle quietness to the virtuous woman's strength. Her strength is not loud or boastful, not competitive in nature. It does not have to be advertised at all, but is seen and felt as she esteems others better than herself.. How about you, dear lady? Have you been tempted to prove to men that you are strong - if not stronger - than them? Strength in themselves is an unattractive quality that women of the feminist movement have placed much emphasis on. The world provokes women to own and to exercise their right of strength and power, yet the fruit of it is quite loud and abrasive! Not so with the strength of the Lord, for it is strength mixed with humility...

Is 30:15, ".....in quietness and confidence shall be your strength...."

This matter of honor is quite important in the life of the virtuous woman. Unlike worldly women, she knows how to carry herself, as we all are exhorted to do in 1 Thessalonians 4:4:

"That every one of you ought to know how to possess his vessel in sanctification and honour."

Because she has first honored the Lord, the virtuous woman has the proper perspective on other things that are honorable in this life as the Word of God teaches her *who* and *what* she should honor. In Romans 13:7, the Bible exhorts us to render honor to whom honor is due. Do you know who you should be honoring in your life today, dear lady??

1 Timothy 1:17, "Now unto the King eternal, immortal, invisible, the only wise God, be honour and glory for ever and ever."

Psalm 26:8 says, "Lord, I have loved the habitation of thy house, and the place where thine honour dwelleth."

Sad to say, but I do not think Christians honor God, His Word, or His house as humbly as they should! They find such choices cramp their style... With that being the case, it would only stand to reason that we are then not honoring God's ways either as carried out in daily life. Honoring others is a rich part of the virtuous woman's character and she is blessed in doing so! Pr 20:3 tells us it is an honor for a man to cease from strife and the virtuous woman is not a meddling woman who steps into arguments easily. She honors the *position* of others in humility (Romans 12:10). Her husband is highly honored by her, for she believes Hebrews 13:4 which states that *marriage* is honorable. The virtuous woman places honor on her marriage because God does!

How about you, dear lady? Are you honoring your marriage today in your heart, and outwardly in the treatment of your husband, or are you viewing it as a curse that has come into your life? We must be clothed with humility to receive honor of God! Because honor is deeply rooted in the virtuous woman's life, she enjoys a precious prayer life that knows no hindrances and receives many answers...

Psalm 91:14-16 says, "Because he hath set his love upon me, therefore will I deliver him: I will set him on high, because he hath known my name. He shall call upon me, and I will answer him: I will be with him in trouble; I will deliver him, and honour him. With long life will I satisfy him, and shew him my salvation."

What rich rewards! No wonder the virtuous woman chose honor as part of her "infit" every day! God honors a life that honors Him. Have your prayers been hindered lately, dear lady? Perhaps there is an area of your life that lacks an attitude of honor; whether toward a particular person, a position of authority, your marriage - the Lord??

Yes, the virtuous woman chooses to wear strength and honor as protective covering every day, and is found still wearing these same spiritual garments in her old age. They never go out of style with God! Consequently, *she rejoices in time to come,* she has a happy future! There will come a day in her old age when she will reflect with comfort that she was not idle or useless when young and that through the Lord's strength she held up under the storms of life. Imagine sitting on the lap of an elderly woman of virtue, hearing the godly stories she will have to tell as a grandmother… Though her outward man perish and her physical beauty fades away, though she may stoop in her walk or need to employ a cane, her inward character remains strong and honorable, for in Christ it is renewed day by day and kept alive forever....

Psalm 73:26, "My flesh and my heart faileth: but God is the strength of my heart and my portion forever."

Future blessings await a woman of virtue and she is promised a day of rejoicing - an eternity of it! Yes, she sows in tears during her lifetime yet *never gives up*, therefore she shall reap in joy! Ladies, we are promised that same day of rejoicing too! Dress for success – make strength and honor part of your style from now on!

THE CONVERSATION OF THE VIRTUOUS WOMAN

Proverbs 31:26

"She openeth her mouth with wisdom; and in her tongue is the law of kindness."

I rarely avoid conviction when reading this verse, for I have said many things in the past that I now regret, and left many things unsaid that I regret as well. A particular ingredient makes an important difference in the speech of a virtuous woman... Wisdom is the very foundation of her strength of character; therefore, it personally escorts every word that ushers forth from her lips. She carefully, prayerfully, thoughtfully, and purposely she chooses each word before giving it away. Each word spoken by the virtuous woman is wrapped in God's wisdom, for the Word of God is her guide in knowing both *when* to speak and *how* to speak. It is the very law of her lips!

Ecclesiastes 3:7b, "...a time to speak and a time to keep silence."

Ladies, are we known for having a reputation for godly articulation? Are you typically hasty with your words or do you ponder them first before giving them away? Are you frequently sorry for the things you have said? Do you weigh your words by HIS Word - the HOLY Bible? God's wisdom will make the ultimate difference in your verbal expressions. It has the power to chase away all those regrets we might have for the improper things we have uttered...

If all that we say,
In a single day;
With never a word left out,
Were printed each night,
In clear black and white;
'T'would prove queer reading, no doubt!

And, then, just suppose,
'Ere our eyes we could close;
We must read the whole record through.
Then wouldn't we sigh,
And wouldn't we try
A great deal less talking to do?

And, I more than half think,
That many a kink
Would be smoother in life's tangled thread,
If half that we say,
In a single day,
Were left forever unsaid.

Proverbs 15:28 says, "The heart of the righteous studieth to answer: but the mouth of the wicked poureth out foolishness."

Proverbs 16:23 says, "The heart of the wise teacheth his mouth, and addeth learning to his lips."

Just because we are women, and just because we are known for our love for conversation does not mean we are expert in our knowledge or use of wise words! Everyone should speak properly and anyone can! The scriptures above instruct us to *study*, to put forth some effort in learning how to speak wisely! Correct use of our tongues happens on purpose - not by accident! YOU are to take responsibility for knowing how to open your mouth! If you've been struggling with appropriate communication, **study!!** As a home schooling mother, I do not allow my children to employ excuses for not knowing answers when they at least know where to find them. Those of you with children in public or private school would also consider your children lazy for not using the resources available to ascertain necessary information to complete their assignments. Why then do we clutch our own list of excuses for oral ignorance when we have the Word of God as our rich and perfect resource - full of wise words - to study from?!
I hope that while your children are getting their lessons in language at school each day, you are getting your education on the subject of knowing how to open your mouth with wisdom! Learn all you can and then teach your children the importance of wise words... We all need God's grammar lessons!

Deut.6:6 & 7, "And these words, which I command thee this day, shall be in thine heart: And thou shalt teach them diligently unto thy children, and shalt talk of them when thou sittest in thine house, and when thou walkest by the way, and when thou liest down, and when thou risest up."

Proverbs 10:32 says, "The lips of the righteous know what is acceptable: but the mouth of the wicked speaketh frowardness."

So often, we engage in conversation that is not wholesome and we do not stop to think first if it is acceptable. Acceptable with whom? With our Lord, of course! Would God consider the words that have been proceeding forth from your heart and out of your body via your lips, *acceptable*? The tongue's great storehouse is the heart… What words have you stored up in your heart that are now flowing out of your lips? The Bible says the righteous should **know** what words the Lord would approve of. It should be the heart's desire of every Christian to utter such things that are pleasing in their heavenly Father's sight and to His ears. Imagine the "noise pollution" that must rise up to the ears of the Lord as He daily listens to the speech of this world and to the speech of His children. Is there a difference between what the world is talking about and what He hears YOU talking about?? Is there any slang on your lips, Christian woman?

Psalm 19:14 says, "Let the words of my mouth, and the meditation of my heart, be acceptable in thy sight, O Lord, my strength, and my redeemer."

What is the meditation of your heart today? I ask because it will have an affect upon your words, ladies! The thought life of a woman of virtue is very instrumental in the language that springs forth from her lips. She knows this and calls upon the Lord for His help and strength to both think and speak wisely, while doing her part of studying how to answer. Are you praying about these two closely related and important character qualities in your life? Guide your thoughts by Philippians 4:8 and your words will follow suit! Our heavenly Father has supplied us with a list of things we must think on. It consists of whatsoever things are true, honest, just, pure, lovely, of good report, any virtue, any praise - can you file *all* your thoughts under these categories? If not, you have been placing them outside of the will of God! Ladies, you must understand that your thought life will give wings to your words... What kinds of words have been flying around at your house? I assure you that if you captured one of those flying words you would be able to attach it to a thought from which it was first born! Guard your thought life diligently; place it in custody of the Holy Spirit, and your words will come under control...

2 Corinthians 10:5, "Casting down imaginations, and every high thing that exalteth itself against the knowledge of God, and bringing into captivity every thought to the obedience of Christ."

When guided by the Word of God, you too, will open your mouth with wisdom! There is no excuse - it is our personal responsibility! If I could travel around this world and be responsible for removing all the thoughts in women's hearts and minds that cause them to sin with their lips, I would have quite a ministry!

Trying to accomplish such a task in my own heart and mind is enough to keep me busy until the Lord returns! Nevertheless, it is not possible for me to do that for you, nor can any of you do that for me. It is a choice we must make for ourselves. We must cast down that which exalts itself against the Lord in our lives and grab hold of that which brings glory and honor to His name. Once wisdom becomes the foundation from which the virtuous woman opens her mouth, we are going to find *kindness* in her tongue. Kindness is the frosting on the cupcake of her every word. There is softness and sweetness in how she says what she says, born of a heart controlled by the Holy Spirit of God. Words of correction sent from her lips are not unpleasant when accompanied by the law of kindness that is in her tongue.

Ecc. 10:12 says, "The words of a wise man's lips are gracious...."

Galatians 5:22, "But the fruit of the Spirit is love, joy, peace, longsuffering, gentleness, goodness, faith..."

Also, a woman of virtue is not a talebearer, not a backbiter, not a brawler, not a slanderer, not a babbler that utters vain words, not a liar, not a flatterer, not an evil whisperer... She let's NO corrupt communication proceed out of her mouth, but that which is good to the use of edifying, that it may minister grace unto the hearers of her words. Her daily conversation is guided by Ephesians 4:29-32. Because the Holy Spirit of God controls her, she does not want to grieve her Lord in any way. The virtuous woman is therefore skilled in the art of godly communication. Many people today, even Christians, lack such an important skill necessary in life! No wonder marriages suffer when such aptitude is abandoned, as husbands and wives neglect the studying of how to answer one another as laid out for them in the Word of God!

Ephesians 4:31, "Let all bitterness, and wrath, and anger, and clamour, and evil speaking be put away from you, with all malice."

Can I ask you a question today, dear lady? What happens when you get angry? Do you verbally vomit your hostility all over the people around you? Do you speak evil things that you later regret? The Bible says to put such words away from you - throw them out! Malice accompanies such ugly, damaging words and it is an ungodly spirit. It is a quality defined as extreme enmity of heart, a disposition to injure others without cause, from mere personal gratification or from a spirit of revenge; unprovoked malignity or spite. Ladies, there is an ungodly spirit that attends such mean words! Keep your hearts clear of garbage so your speech can be pure. In Isaiah 53:7, the Bible tells us that when Jesus was oppressed and afflicted he opened not His mouth. What about you and I, what do we do under hardship? Sad to say, but that is not usually our testimony, is it? I daresay we open WIDE our mouths and pour out rubbish! If Christ dwells in our hearts by faith, then we have the ability to yield to the Holy Spirit and react as He did under oppression and affliction.

Verse 32 of Ephes. 4 goes on to say, "...and be ye kind one to another..."

Here is God's therapy for those who find themselves faced with the calamity of oral sewage. Filthy words proceed from corruption in the speaker… They further corrupt the minds and manners of those who hear them and baste them with the dung of our soiled hearts. Christians should beware of all such behavior in themselves! It is our duty to think gravely, and caution believers by the dialogue they exchange. The Lord orders us to be *kind* one to another! Consider how kind the Lord was toward us, how He forgave us, died for us, how He spoke words of love to us!

Corrupt communications that stir up evil desires and lusts and grieve the Spirit of God should be put far from us! Kind actions produce kind words. Let us open our mouths with wisdom and give others the benefit of experiencing the *kindness* of wise words.

Luke 6:35b, "….for he is kind unto the unthankful and to the evil."

In closing, I want to tell you that the virtuous woman talks to herself!! Are any of you out there in the habit of doing this? Do not worry; you are not crazy – that is, as long as you guide your "self-talk" by the Word of God...

Ephesians 5:19 & 20 says, "Speaking to yourselves in psalms and hymns and spiritual songs, singing and making melody in your heart to the Lord. Giving thanks always for all things unto God and the Father in the name of our Lord Jesus Christ."

Ladies, I hope these are the kinds of things you are muttering to yourselves each and every day within your homes and your hearts! Self-talk can be very negative and damaging; be careful that it stays under the control of the Holy Spirit as well. He will always tell you the truth! Your own ears should be hearing you speak words of wisdom and kindness - not defeat and discouragement! Speak to yourself wisely, dear lady! After all, the Bible says a man has joy by the answer of his mouth, amen? How happy do you really want to be? How happy do you think the virtuous woman was? It had a great deal to do with her conversation…

THIS TONGUE OF MINE

Oh; Spirit of the living God
Control this tongue of mine,
No knife is quite so sharp as words,
Yet words can be divine.
A tongue not yielded to God's will
Can stir up awful strife.
Lord use this tongue of mine today
To speak thy Words of life.

I want my tongue to sing God's praise,
To tell His love for me,
To speak God's Holy name in prayer
And thanks for Calvary.
Lord help me that this tongue of mine
Shall speak Thy word in love
That what I say will be Thy will
Directed from above.

Oh; Holy Spirit, faithful guide
This tongue of mine inspire
That only words that please the Lord
Shall be my heart's desire.
So may I lead some soul to Christ
By spoken words or songs.
Then as God leads, do not forget
My tongue to Him belongs.

THE VIGILANCE OF THE VIRTUOUS WOMAN

Proverbs 31:27

"She looketh well to the ways of her household, and eateth not the bread of idleness."

We find here that vigilance is part of the virtuous woman's character. She directs her intellectual eye toward her home and views all aspects of it with painstaking detail. She works conscientiously to establish and maintain routine of a prudent nature. Because she looketh *well* to the ways of her household, she is on the lookout for the possibility of someone in her home that might be sneaking a portion of the bread of idleness! She is the overseer; the guide that carries out the king's wishes in their home. Her husband has delegated authority to her in certain areas and as a result, she assigns duties to bring about the proper running of the household. As a faithful manager, she refuses to sneak any of that tempting bread of idleness for herself! As a mother, the virtuous woman ensures that the children are constantly involved in the work that needs to be done in the home. She does not insist upon doing it all herself, neither does she place the entire load on their shoulders, but understands the wisdom in training up children to assume a range of responsibilities as part of the family. She sees to it that when they carry out a task, they do it *well*. That means the virtuous woman does not make allowances for flimsy excuses concerning the lack of quality in their work. Neither does she make excuses for their behavior in order to protect them from punishment or accountability.

Yes, a woman of virtue is meticulous; extremely careful; giving close attention to every detail. If a job is not done right, she makes her children go back and do it again, for doing things *well* is important! The word "well" means in a proper manner, sufficient, thoroughly, so as to require no alteration. Their tears or cries for mercy do not manipulate the virtuous woman, or even their cute little cherub faces, but her love for them requires that they do the hard thing. She has given them *reasonable* duties and added a sensible schedule to the carrying out of those duties. Might I add, the virtuous woman is consistent in overseeing of the affairs of her household and sees to it that she is **respected** in that role! She does not permit her children to speak disrespectfully to her nor does she argue with them about their responsibilities.

Matthew 15:4, "For God commanded, saying, Honour thy father and mother: and, He that curseth father or mother, let him die the death."

Ladies, do not let your children run you or your home – YOU do it! For example, many children today dictate what is eaten at meals and even the hour they will eat. "I'm not hungry now!" Mother answers, "Okay Johnny, you just tell "mummy" when you want to eat, sweetheart, and tell "mummy" what you want and she will get it for you." The problem with that is, Johnny will grow up bossing "mummy" around because "mummy" is not looking *well* to the ways of her household!! She is eating the bread of idleness... Little Johnny is the one in charge! Johnny tells "mummy" and daddy when he will go to bed and when he will be home from a friend's house and what he wants purchased for him, and on and on the cycle goes! Ladies, looking *well* to your household means that YOU are in control, not your children and their fleshly desires!!

Proverbs 19:18, "Chasten thy son while there is hope, and let not thy soul spare for his crying."

So dear mother, are you able to make decisions without your little tyke pitching a fit, or have you let him or her become a monster and surrendered to limiting yourself and your activities because of it? Have you been idle in the area of child training and discipline? Looking *well* to the ways of your household includes dealing with the improper behavior of those within it. Don't turn a deaf ear to your children's fit throwing, don't be **idle** in your discipline - deal with the situation properly and maintain management of your household. Look *well* to these issues!

Proverbs 29:15, ".... a child left to himself bringeth his mother to shame."

The shame a mother is brought to is a result of her own idleness in the life of her child! She has chosen it for herself by refusing to do anything about the behavior of her children... If a child left to himself brings his mother to shame, does a mother left to herself bring her children to shame?? You bet she does! She also brings her husband to shame as well as dishonors the name of the Lord Jesus Christ if she is a Christian! Are you idle today, dear lady? Idleness is a dangerous position to be in! The virtuous woman refuses to eat of such bread. She has no appetite for inactivity or ignoring what needs to be dealt with...

Eccles. 10:18, "By much slothfulness the building decayeth; and through idleness of the hands the house droppeth through."

Have you ever scheduled yourself a day of "idleness" as therapy for living a demanding life? Be careful, you might develop taste buds for such a lifestyle! Persistent idleness should not be permitted. A woman of virtue does not want to train her heart to enjoy such bread. She has refused to eat of the devil's bakery.

According to the Bible, Satan has many types of bread to choose from... There is the bread of deceit, which is sweet; the bread of sorrows, the bread of wickedness, the bread of mourners and many others listed in the Word of God. Ladies, the virtuous woman has an appetite for the bread of **Heaven**, the bread of **Life**, and eats regularly of spiritual fullness! This is the bread that satisfies her soul and protects her from developing an appetite for "loafing around."

John 6:48-51 says, "I am that bread of life. Your fathers did eat manna in the wilderness, and are dead. This is the bread which cometh down from heaven, that a man may eat thereof, and not die. I am the living bread which came down from heaven: if any man eat of this bread, he shall live for ever: and the bread that I will give is my flesh, which I will give for the life of the world."

When you are idle, you are in a position for the enemy to come in and take control. You have not chosen a purpose for your life and so he will come along, capture you, and fulfill his own purposes! In Mt. 20:3,6, the idle are found in the marketplaces, much like people today, aimlessly wandering up and down the malls, window shopping and overloading their charge cards with debt for lack of something better to do. In 1 Tim. 5:13, the idle are said to wander from house to house - something they learned to do when they were young....

When a person develops a wandering lifestyle, his lips follow his feet and meander their way into the business of other people. Be careful moms, that you are not so busy running hither and yon that your daughters are developing an appetite for being OUT of the house more than they are for being IN the house! Will your daughter and or daughters be content to be at home based on the upbringing you have provided her/them? Are you looking *well* to the molding of their hearts, or feeding them the bread of idleness little by little, day by day?

Ezekiel 16:49, "Behold, this was the iniquity of thy sister Sodom, pride, fulness of bread, and abundance of idleness was in her and in her daughters, neither did she strengthen the hand of the poor and needy."

As homeschoolers, we have more liberty to be on the go, running our children here and there to music lessons, sporting events, horseback riding lessons, swimming lessons, art classes, chess club etc. Though all these things are good activities for our children, are we training them that home is just a pit stop and not a place to love to BE?? Funny, but we call ourselves HOMEschoolers and we are rarely HOME! We ought to call ourselves ROAMschoolers instead, with such nomadic behavior!

I don't know if you've picked up on this or not, but I've become aware of the fact that many young children discuss amid themselves what sort of a car they are going to purchase when they are older - even the girls! I have heard teenage girls chatting about colors and styles of cars that they personally prefer over others. How do they know so much about cars – and why?? Obviously, they have given this matter some consideration to have already formed an opinion. I don't remember that ever being an issue for me or my girlfriends. Then I got to thinking - this generation has spent more time in a car than probably anywhere else! Not only is more time spent in a car than at home, but probably more time is spent in a vehicle than even in the house of God.... I am so thankful my mother did not have a car, for I was always at home while growing up. Today I prefer to be in my home to anywhere else, except for church. Mothers, balance your time wisely - look *well* to the ways of your household!! Be sure that you are not coaching idleness in subtle ways. Consider what future struggles may arise because of your daily choices to constantly be on the go!

Jeremiah 14:10, "Thus saith the Lord unto this people, <u>Thus have they loved to wander</u>, they have not refrained their feet, therefore the Lord doth not accept them; he will now remember their iniquity, and visit their sins."

Spurgeon said of idleness; "I am not the only one that condemns the idle; for once when I was going to give our minister a pretty long list of the sins of one of our people whom he was asking after, I began with: "He's dreadfully lazy." "That's enough," said the old gentleman; "all sorts of sins are in that one."

What course are you on today, dear lady? What tendencies are showing up at your house? Have you taken the time to watch closely over such matters and method of life and conduct? Are you meticulous or reckless concerning the ways of your household? Ladies, let's purpose in our hearts to look *well* to the habits that are developing within our homes and refuse to partake of the bread of idleness. Let us commit to doing what needs to be done, what GOD says ought to be done! Let us keep our lives from being filled with vain activity and fill our homes with handfuls of purpose!

1 Peter 5:8, "Be sober, be vigilant…"

THE CHILDREN OF THE VIRTUOUS WOMAN

Proverbs 31:28, Part 1

"Her children arise up, and call her blessed, her husband also, and he praiseth her."

Did you realize that this is the first specific mention of children in this chapter? Before this verse, the Bible spoke of "her household". Now we observe that motherhood was an important part of who the virtuous woman was. It is not, in her mind, an unpleasant role to be "stuck" with, but parenthood is an extension of this woman's nurturing nature, and her heart's yearning. Being a mother is more than just an "experience" that the virtuous woman squeezes in around her career, it is a passion that brings great joy to her life! She values this blessed role, for she knows what the Word of God has to say about motherhood. What the Lord places significance upon, she too gives high appraisal....

Psalm 127:3, "Lo, children are an heritage of the Lord; and the fruit of the womb is his reward."

Psalm 113:9, "He maketh the barren woman to keep house, and to be a joyful mother of children."

Isaiah 8:18, "Behold, I and the children whom the Lord hath given me are for signs and for wonders in Israel from the Lord of hosts, which dwelleth in mount Zion."

Ladies, did you notice that in the three verses above the Lord is the giver of children? Yes, He desires that we have them! It is God's design that His people raise up godly seed. Joyful mothers and their saintly children are to be for signs and wonders in this lost and dying world. Signs of what? Of God's grace! Yes, our children ought to capture the attention of lost people – for *good* reasons, not bad ones… When is the last time you detected upright, honorable children outside of your church family? When is the last time you came across a woman who was a truly *joyful* mother? Is that the title you would give yourself today, dear lady? Sad to say, but many mothers and their children are for signs and wonders of the incorrect way of living rather than the correct! The world has subtracted from the value of parenting children in it's promotion of abortion and daycare systems, and Christians have stood by and allowed it to happen - even contributed to the promotion of such conduct! Children all over this world have been herded together into daycare systems, much like cattle in a barn, to be mass fed and educated, forsaken by parents that have gladly given them over - even Christian parents! Yes, the children that GOD gave THEM to raise! Oh, women will gladly take the *experience* of motherhood – but minus the *expenditure*…

Genesis 33:5 says, "And he lifted up his eyes, and saw the women and the children; and said, <u>Who are those with thee?</u> And he said, The children which God hath graciously given thy servant."

Are your children with you today, dear lady?? The virtuous woman was an example to the world that her children were highly valued; they were precious ones worth staying home for and raising herself! She acknowledges that God graciously gave them to her and she kept them WITH her as the verse above points out.

A virtuous woman gives of herself repeatedly for the good of her children and for God's glory. Notice in our opening scripture the direction the Bible says her children take... God's Word says they ARISE UP. Ladies, children benefit, they blossom, and they excel because of the sacrificial role of such a God fearing woman in their lives! The virtuous woman does not substitute holding the precious little hands of her children in exchange for clutching a briefcase... Nor does she try to pass them off to others just to get them out of her hair! What message are you sending this world concerning motherhood, Christian woman? Is your life convincing others it's a role not worth very much, or is it showing them that God's grace is sufficient and the blessings of motherhood abundant and rewarding? How valuable do you think your children feel to their mother today? Is there anything you are placing more importance upon than their existence in this world? Is that replacement really worth more than what God says your children are worth?? Ladies, we have our children for such a short time, we ought to sacrifice our lives for them, not their lives for ourselves!

Romans 12:1, "I beseech you therefore, brethren, by the mercies of God, that ye present your bodies a living sacrifice, holy, acceptable unto God, which is your reasonable service."

Now, you may be wondering about how to get your children to *arise up*.... You may be asking yourself, "Am I doing the necessary things in raising my children as the virtuous woman did to see their lives take an upward direction; that they walk the path that leads them to higher ground?" Just as a woman of virtue is familiar with God's perspective on children, she is also knowledgeable concerning God's way of raising those children He so graciously gave her. The Giver Of Children also furnished us a manual to submit to in caring for our offspring; a sacred book called the Bible!

The contents are not from Dr. Spock, not Dr. Dobson, not Dear Abbey, not even Dr. Laura, but written by our heavenly FATHER, the Author and Finisher of our faith! He is a perfect parent and the One most qualified to turn to for help. Why would we not rely upon what God has to say about raising our children? Have you been looking to His Word for parenting wisdom, dear lady, or has your nose been in another book, another man or woman's method?

Eccles. 12:12-13, "And further, by these, my son, be admonished: of making many books there is no end; and much study is a weariness of the flesh. Let us hear the conclusion of the whole matter: Fear God, and keep his commandments: for this is the whole duty of man."

Ladies, in hopes of bringing our children up in this world, we must make certain that we do not forsake our parental duties as laid out in the Word of God....

Deut.6: 6&7 says, "And these words, which I command thee this day, shall be in thine heart: And thou shalt teach them diligently unto thy children, and shalt talk of them when thou sittest in thine house, and when thou walkest by the way, and when thou liest down, and when thou risest up."

First, we find in this verse that the Word of God should find entrance into our own hearts! Then we are to thoroughly teach them to our children as we have been commanded. That means we ought to have spiritual discussions with our children in order to educate, train, guide, and counsel them from the Holy Scriptures. When? "When thou sittest in thine house." How do you plan on obeying God in this matter if you're never home?? On the other hand, if you are at home, no such dialogue will be come to pass between parent and child if you are always so busy with household tasks that you never *sit* with your children! When is the last time you did so?

Psalm 46:10, "Be still, and know that I am God...."

Mothers, if you desire to see your children excel in life, then throughout the day, wherever your feet may take you, you must teach your children of the Lord. There are so many things God has for us every day that He wants us to see and then point out to our children! Let me ask you this question; how much do you notice when you are running around like a chicken with your head cut off? (I love that old expression!) Have you ever tried to talk when you are running? It is difficult, isn't it? Can our children keep up with our fast pace when their steps are naturally smaller? Not without difficulty... Is it possible that in our hurriedness we are missing many of life's lessons the Lord has for us to learn and share? Could it be that children suffer because their parents are always running here and there? It is no secret that you make more mistakes when you are in a hurry... Ladies, your children might have some important questions to ask you about life, about the Lord, but they cannot because you are dragging them all over God's creation at 90 miles an hour! Stop, look, and listen to their tender hearts, and to the Lord! Let us slow down for their sakes, for God's sake in their lives! Instead of running, let us walk for a change...

Psalm 101:2, "I will behave myself wisely in a perfect way. O when wilt thou come unto me? I will WALK within my house with a perfect heart."

In closing, mothers who do not place proper significance upon their children should find it no surprise when they reap what they have sown. A virtuous woman has a strong testimony before her children, her own little congregation. There is nothing that gratifies children more than a mother who values them! This is what provokes them to call her "blessed" – to return the value and place it lovingly upon her head.

Yes, the woman that made them face up to hard things is considered a blessing in their lives, not a curse! She is hallowed of her children for her faith in God and her faithfulness to them. It is the result of a lifetime of love and sacrifice on her part. Yes, the influence of truly virtuous mothers is without comparison… Her children arise up, yet they never forget her!

Hebrews 2:13, "And again, I will put my trust in him. And again, Behold I and the children which God hath given me."

THE RECOGNITION OF THE VIRTUOUS WOMAN

Proverbs 31:28, Part 2

"Her children arise up, and call her blessed; her husband also, and he praiseth her."

Like her children, the man who is connected to a woman of virtue is also elevated as a result of her presence and role in the home, her companionship in his life. We already know that he held a place of honor and respect in the community and sat among the elders, that she freed him up to be used of God. A proper wife is her husband's better half, his heart's delight and treasure. He says to her: "I shall in thee most happy be. In thee, my choice, I do rejoice. In thee, I find content of mind. He finds his earthly heaven in her company... She is the light of his home and the comfort of his soul...

Proverbs 18:22, "Whoso findeth a wife findeth a good thing, and obtaineth favour of the Lord."

Indeed, the husband of the virtuous woman has become a strong man; one who is not for sale, not easily persuaded, nor ashamed to say no with emphasis. He is one who will condemn wrong in friend or foe and in his own life also. He has a proper view of himself in the light of God's Word and is not braggadocios. He knows the message of God and tells it. His conscience is steady and not swayed off the mark. He is one who courageously stands for right in the face of opposition. This strong man does not run from the hard task, but does what is necessary - without fear of failing. How is this so? His virtuous wife *believes* in him! He also knows his business and tends to it. He is not too lazy to work, nor too proud to help with the least little task. Through his wife's patience and support, he has learned to be a lover - apart from embarrassment. Hence, he easily and wisely loves his wife and children.

Yet, in spite of all his strengths, this man also has weaknesses. His wife, he knows, can see them - and has seen them, at times when no one else is aware of them. What has she done with the knowledge of these weaknesses, these shortcomings of her husband's? The virtuous woman has hidden them behind her love and commitment to him and her faith in God! His heart safely trusts in her so that he shall have no need of spoil.... This man is commanded by the Word of God in Gen. 2:24 to leave his father and mother and cleave unto his wife. He has been commanded by the Word of God to love his wife in Ephesians 5:25. The virtuous woman has made God's commandments an *easy* task for her husband, not a chore to face with drudgery! He knows from Pr. 5:18 that he is to rejoice with the wife of his youth, and from Ecc. 9:9 that he is to live joyfully with her *all* the days of his life. Have you made this a difficult undertaking for your husband, dear lady? Are you trying to make his life miserable because you are convinced he has done that to yours?? You see, the virtuous woman did not expect to find a perfect man! If you come across a man without any faults, incapable of mistakes, never having estimated wrongly, his patience never having been agitated, flawless in speech, in disposition, in behavior - please don't marry him!! It wouldn't be fair… What would you do with a perfect man, you who are not perfect yourself?? How dare we try to extract such behavior of our husbands when we are not angels ourselves! In other words, there are **no** perfect men and **no** perfect women! Even Adam and Eve, residents of Paradise, were without merit of their own. Ladies, it's time we removed unreasonable expectations and loved our husbands as we should, thereby making it easy for them to love us, not more difficult! As I was riding in the car with my daughter the other night, I remarked to her that she followed the drivers in front of her too closely, not permitting enough room for their mistakes, thereby placing herself in more danger. As soon as those words came out of my mouth, the Lord used that illustration to prick my heart and point out that as wives, we are guilty of the same thing! We "tailgate" our husbands, never leaving any room in their lives for them to grow in grace and knowledge of the Lord. Have you ever tried to drive with someone tailgating you? It is very annoying and distracting, not to mention downright rude! A virtuous woman cultivates her husband's heart and makes it a field of praise... Give your man some space, dear lady; stop riding him! Give GOD the space He needs to lead him in this life. Follow at a *proper* distance! Praise is a natural attitude of *grateful* hearts. A heart that is full of praise knows no hindrances within... The virtuous woman's husband was a satisfied and contented man with his wife, no need of his was unmet. He easily and eagerly praised her. To say wonderful, pleasant things of her did not feel "phony" to him. Other men he was sitting near in the gates of the city may have been grumbling and murmuring about their wives, but the virtuous woman's husband could utter nothing but public appreciation for his bride. She was a crown to him and he wore that crown with pride.... He walked well so as not to cause his crown to fall... That which was precious to him was not going to be lost! Generally, we enthusiastically praise those who admire us... This man gave honor to the crown that brought honor to him, to his position, and to his life.

Isaiah 62:5, "For as a young man marrieth a virgin, so shall thy sons marry thee: and as the bridegroom rejoiceth over the bride, so shall thy God rejoice over thee."

Yes, the virtuous woman's husband even praised his wife before his children. He reminded them of what a wonderful mother they had, and in turn taught them to praise her too! (She also trained them to praise their father!!)

Not only did he praise his wife to others, he voiced his praise to her personally so that she knew how he felt about her. This man wanted his virtuous wife to know how grateful he was for the intricate part she played in his life. He wanted her to know that without her, life would not be the same for him. He would be incomplete! He is grateful for her loyalty in life's difficulties, and through his failures. A woman of virtue has faith and courage enough to submit herself to an imperfect man while he submits to a perfect God. In the end, her husband felt she was more than he deserved, more than he ever hoped for. Have you given your husband *good* cause to praise you, dear wife??

"Oh, let her come from out the lands
Of womanhood - not fairy isles!
And let her come with woman's hands
And woman's eyes of tears and smiles,
With woman's hopefulness and grace
Of patience lighting up her face,
And let her diadem be wrought
Of kindly deed and prayerful thought,
That ever over all distress
May beam the light of cheerfulness;
And let her feet be brave to fare
The labyrinths of doubt and care,
That following my own may find
The path to Heaven God designed.
Oh, let her come like this to me -

My bride - my bride that is to be! As seen in Song of Solomon 7:1-10, the bridegroom praised his wife for her physical beauty. No detail went unnoticed in his eyes as she kept herself beautiful for him. His desire was toward her and her only. He was ravished always with her love... Likewise, we must ensure that we are physically attractive to our husbands! It should be our heart's desire to bring them *visual* pleasure! I can guarantee you this - if you don't, someone else will! Because God designed them that way, men are visual creatures - do not punish them for that... Have you let yourself fall apart, or are you doing all you can to keep yourself nice-looking for your husband? I think you'd all agree the temptations of this world are strong; why make it easier for your man to look the other way?? Not only was her physical beauty praised, the husband also praised his wife for her spiritual beauty, those inward qualities which he knew were of great price in the sight of God according to 1 Peter 3:3-4, "....even the ornament of a meek and quiet spirit, which is in the sight of God of great price." Husbands take pleasure in the beauty of a meek and quiet spirit dwelling within his wife! You see, Ladies, this woman's spiritual beauty was her Christlikeness of spirit since the Savior came to live within her heart. Jesus is the very center of all recognition she receives... Through His Son, God deposits within each of us an inward beauty that grows daily, but only through our willingness to subject ourselves to our Lord and to our husbands can we similarly be accredited as was the virtuous woman...

Ezekiel 16:14 says, "And thy renown went forth among the heathen for thy beauty: for it was perfect through my comeliness, which I had put upon thee, saith the Lord God."

Yes, this was the beauty that all who came in contact with recognized first and foremost - the outstanding character that her husband and children praised her for.

Ladies, we can all be adorned with such loveliness of heart - all we have to do is yield to the Lord and the Spirit of God can be detected. Who can find a virtuous woman, for her price is far above rubies... Can your family testify that they have found one in you?

THE SUPERIORITY OF THE VIRTUOUS WOMAN

Proverbs 31:29

"Many daughters have done virtuously, but thou excellest them all."

The word "excellest" means to go beyond, surpass, exceed. The Bible says *many* women have done well in the areas we have discussed over the course of this study, but ladies, many is not *most*, amen? I hope you are determined to be one of the few women who go *beyond* in godly matters! Are you content with yourself today, or is there a desire within you to surpass the norm?? A woman of virtue is a lady whose very being is filled with supremacy. Fineness permeates her every thought, word, and deed. Scores of Christian women can execute virtuous acts, going through religious motions while carrying out their daily duties and responsibilities, yet the virtuous woman goes further than the typical performance. Her **heart** is in everything she does! Moreover, within her heart dwells excellency… She spends her life contributing to the excellence of her husband, her children, her home, her church and church family, the community etc. This increases the blessing she is to society and her value in God's eyes, as well as in man's eyes. Her own reputation is enlarged upon forgetting self! Here is a woman who excels, soars, and skyrockets by putting herself last! Yes, all the while the virtuous woman is busy building the supremacy of others, she is building worth into her own life through becoming a servant... Not typically the world's way of excelling, is it, ladies? The world says, "Look out for number one!" Who might that be? They are referring to none other than *self*… Praise the Lord a woman of virtue chooses to esteem others better than herself and travels the path of excellence God's way!

1 Cor. 14:12, "….seek that ye may excel to the edifying of the church."

In looking at Genesis 49:3-4, where Jacob is speaking to his son Reuben, the Bible says, "Unstable as water, thou shalt not excel..." Ladies, the virtuous woman is steadfast and sure and a woman of godly purpose. This purpose prevents her from becoming unstable.

She is not double minded and knows from the Word of God that a double minded man is unstable in *all* his ways, not just some of them. (James 1:8) She governs herself properly and refuses to halt between two opinions, as many are guilty of doing today. Her choices and decisions are not dictated by her feelings...(Phil. 1:10) She does not entangle herself with things that would bring her under bondage or immobilize her. She is consistent and intent on seeing things through until the finish - that end being *excellency*! High merit will not settle for less... How about you? Have you been unstable in your walk with the Lord, dear lady? Is your Christian life a pattern of "on again, off again"? If you do not fix yourself upon God, you will not thrive, for excellency is born of stability.

1 Chron. 16:30, "Fear before him, all the earth: the world also shall be stable, that it be not moved."

In 1 Kings 4:30 the Bible says that Solomon's wisdom *excelled* the wisdom of all the children of the east country and all the wisdom of Egypt. In 1 Kings 10:23 the Bible says that King Solomon *exceeded* all the kings of the earth. In 2 Chronicles 1:1 scripture states, "And Solomon the son of David was strengthened in his kingdom, and the Lord his God was with him, and magnified him *exceedingly*." When Daniel was brought before King Belshazzar in Daniel 5:13 & 14, he was told by the king that he had heard of him and that light and understanding and *excellent* wisdom was found in him. In Daniel 6:3 we see that Daniel was preferred above the presidents and princes for the *excellent* spirit within him. What is the secret to such excellency in the lives of these Christians? Ladies, the excellency spoken of in scripture is a consequence of the presence and control of God in our lives. The Lord is the reason for any soundness we exhibit, the very root of our virtues! In our pride, we think **our** talents and skills make us excellent. Nothing could be further from the truth!

Some even think they cannot achieve excellency because the same talents and skills present in others are not present in them. This too, is an untruth! We have no excellency of ourselves apart from Christ, and the sooner we accept this truth the more excellent we will become! Break up those lies the devil has been feeding you and within will dawn the realization that you and I can do ALL things <u>through Christ</u> which strengtheneth us, and only through Him! No matter who we are, we **can** become virtuous women and *excel*, regardless of our weaknesses, our upbringing, our circumstances etc. The virtuous woman accepted this truth and the Lord magnified her testimony!

2 Cor. 4:7, "But we have this treasure in earthen vessels, that the excellency of the power may be of God, <u>and not of us</u>."

Yes, excellency is the result of wisdom - GOD'S wisdom - residing in our hearts in the person of the Holy Spirit. As we yield to God's good and holy judgment, then comes excellency - it's that simple! Without God's wisdom, there could be no excellency! Lean not unto your own understanding, dear lady, for you will surely die without wisdom if that is the case. The Bible exhorts us to lean upon the Word of God, to acknowledge Him in *all* our ways and we'll be stable in *all* our ways! To forsake His Word is to forsake excellency…

Proverbs 22:20, "Have not I written to thee excellent things in counsels and knowledge.."

1 Cor. 12:31, "..and yet shew I unto you a more excellent way."

Not only does the Lord yearn for you and I to become virtuous women, He desires us to excel beyond even that! What will you do with the excellency of words that were written for your improvement?
Will you love them, retain them and obey them - or simply waste them?? Are you choosing for yourself a more *excellent* way - God's way, or your own way…

Proverbs 17:27b, "…a man of understanding is of an *excellent* spirit."

Psalm 119:167 says, "My soul hath kept thy precepts and thy testimonies, and I love them *exceedingly*."

Let me ask you this question - do you personally believe that the Word of God is excellent? Do you love it *exceedingly,* by placing high honor upon it? Excellency remains as long as we keep the Word before our eyes... When is the last time you read your Bible?? Are you consistent about it? Do you count all things but loss for the *excellency* of the knowledge of Christ Jesus your Lord? (Phil. 3:8) Ladies, we serve an EXCELLENT God! Why do we turn aside from such magnificence??

Job 37:23a, "Touching the Almighty, we cannot find him out: he is excellent in power, in judgement, and in plenty of justice...."

Psalm 8:9, "O Lord our Lord, how excellent is thy name in all the earth!"

Psalm 36:7, "How excellent is thy lovingkindness, O God! therefore the children of men put their trust under the shadow of thy wings."

In closing, we must remember that Christ's name exceeds all names. It is an excellent name, and there is power of excellency available through His name! What kind of a name have you made for yourself as a child of God, dear lady? Could you be titled a virtuous woman?

I'll be honest with you, I know some good Christian women, but very few *great* ones… A good name is rather to be chosen the Bible says. Hence, a superior testimony is something we pick for ourselves. Perhaps you have been feeling like you could never be a Proverbs 31 woman, that you could never exceed the state of your personhood today. Maybe you have lost ground in some areas you used to excel in as a Christian woman. There are no impossibilities with the Lord, and no need for lost causes. We serve an *excellent* God; the Lord has done everything He could through Christ to make it possible for you and I to go far beyond, to surpass what we ever thought possible!   However, the decision is ours to become distinguished above the usual attainments. His excellency can become our excellency - if we want it bad enough! The trouble is, many women do not want any more virtue than they already have, if they have any at all! Today, why don't you purpose to do more than just go through life smugly - why not endeavor to stand out for your Lord and Savior? Yield to improvement and a superior walk with God; add excellency to your existence!

THE INFATUATION OF THE VIRTUOUS WOMAN

Proverbs 31:30

"Favor is deceitful, and beauty is vain: but a woman that feareth the Lord, she shall be praised."

Beauty, in the physical sense, is perceived by the eye and is pleasing to the senses. Yet, beauty in itself is not proof of wisdom and goodness… In fact, a man who makes his choice of wife by a woman's beauty is merely deceived by it! Proverbs 6:25 says, "Lust not after her beauty in thine heart..." Lusting after a woman's beauty is a simple thing for a man to do, and many men have been destroyed by a woman's good looks; therefore, we must train our boys to identify a truly beautiful woman. Seen things are temporal, unseen things are eternal, and the two are vastly different! True beauty is the fear of the Lord reigning in the heart - the beauty of the *soul*, and it lasts forever! One cannot perceive true beauty until we understand its uses, until a woman's purpose is known… I hope that as mothers we are training our boys not to be mislead by a woman's pleasant appearance but to look beyond at the **heart** of that woman, at the lure of her character. By the way, are you modeling true beauty, dear mother, in order that you might help your son/sons to spot a truly lovely woman? Likewise ladies, in training our young girls, we must also emphasize the importance and value of inward beauty above the outward and prevent them from spending more time on the one than the other, for physical beauty is a false trust…

Ezekiel 16:15 says, "But thou didst trust in thine own beauty..."

How many of you women trusted in this very thing while growing up? I'll admit to you that I did! I was always complimented for my physical features and I soon learned how to use my appearance in a most improper way to receive attention. I trusted in beauty to get my own way.... Be careful that you do not compliment only the outward appearance of your daughters or the young ladies you may know!

The world places a high value upon good looks and many Christian women and young girls have been deceitfully convinced that this outward beauty is what matters most. Hence, we fall prey to the same worldly ideas on the subject and forsake God's value system for beauty. He says the hidden man is the MOST significant....

1 Peter 3:4, "But let it be the <u>hidden man of the heart</u>, in that which is not corruptible, even the ornament of a meek and quiet spirit, which is in the sight of God of great price."

Are any of you still trusting in your physical beauty to get you through this life, to get you praise, recognition, or power? Have you been infatuated with yourself all this time? Perhaps you have begun to discover that outward beauty fades.... I certainly have! For instance, we have been blessed with two boys and only one daughter, who at this time is a beautiful 18 year old young lady... In December, I celebrated my 42nd birthday, and as the two of us were in the bathroom the other day, I noticed in the mirror the growing physical contrast between my daughter and I. One flower is blooming and the other is fading, amen? :-) Perhaps some of you women with teenage daughters can identify with what I am talking about. Those of you with younger girls will soon experience this same realization. I think this is the main reason that many women experience a "mid-life crisis" and become so depressed... They have come face to face with the fact that they have trusted in something that fades away, a false trust placed in their physical attributes and their youth.

Ezekiel 28:17. " Thine heart was lifted up because of thy beauty, thou hast corrupted thy wisdom by reason of thy brightness...."

Proverbs 16:18, "Pride goeth before destruction, and an haughty spirit before a fall."

What do these women have to face the future with when they have spent so many years focused on the outward, only to find they are now bankrupt inwardly?? How vain... I hope that each woman reading this devotion today is not headed for such a crisis! Through a proper relationship with the Lord, there need be no crisis in our lives, amen? Ladies, there will always be someone younger than you, someone skinnier than you, someone who is more shapely, someone whose hair is longer and more attractive, someone whose eyes are brighter, someone whose complexion is clearer, someone whose nose is smaller than yours, someone whose legs don't have varicose veins (ugh!) and on and on it goes. Instead of making it our life's goal to be the most physically attractive, we ought to yearn for the One who is most beautiful of all....

Psalm 27:4, "One thing have I desired of the Lord, that will I seek after; that I may dwell in the house of the Lord all the days of my life, to behold the beauty of the Lord, and to enquire in his temple."

What happens to you when faced with the stark realization of aging, dear lady? You *will* grow old and your beauty *will* fade.... What will happen as the compliments you once received dwindle with your looks? Search your heart today - have you been trusting in your beauty, your outward form? It's a *false* trust - come to terms with it right now and place your trust in Christ and the beauty He alone can fill you with; an inner beauty that will never fade, to be praised by the Lord for all of eternity!

2 Cor. 4:16, "For which cause we faint not; but though our outward man perish, yet the inward man is renewed day by day."

You may not believe me, but most men and women truly think themselves beautiful, they are infatuated with themselves. In fact, they may not realize HOW beautiful they really think they are until the preaching of the Word is upon them....

Psalm 39:11 says, "When thou with rebukes dost correct man for iniquity, thou makest his beauty to consume away like a moth: surely every man is vanity."

Yes, we are content within ourselves and find ourselves quite attractive, often commending ourselves inwardly. But when the Word of God sheds light upon our ugliness - our sin - and magnifies it, we become most disturbed, and very angry at the preacher for placing the mirror of truth before our eyes! Why? Because we have come face to face with our vanity in light of the Scriptures! Our *good* opinion of ourselves has been shattered.... Who enjoys finding a new blemish, a new wrinkle, a new age spot?! Not me! We prefer to remain beautiful in our own eyes but God wants us beautiful in HIS eyes! Don't deprive yourself of sound judgement... Do not resist when the Lord reveals your unattractive qualities to you, those unsightly flaws, those *sins* of yours. He wants to replace your imperfections with the beauty of the character of Christ! Such beauty is what the holy women of old times had a propensity for, as seen in 1 Peter 3:5...

"For after this manner in the old time the holy women also, who trusted in God, adorned themselves..."

Ladies, if it was good enough for the holy women of old time to adorn themselves with the fear of the Lord, then it is good enough for us today! Our God is the same yesterday, today, and forever, the Bible says. Though man may have his worldly opinion of what is attractive, God's opinion of true beauty has not changed, nor will it! The beauty of the virtuous woman is her holiness of character before the Lord.

Psalm 96:9, "O worship the Lord in the beauty of holiness: fear before him, all the earth."

The other day in our study of Proverbs 31, we looked at how the husband and children of the virtuous woman were affected by her and how they commended her. Their human praise was her earthly reward. However, the Bible says there is coming a day of heavenly praise as well! Will you be in a position to receive any?? In possessing the fear of the Lord we have the assurance of future praise - praise of God for a life that was well pleasing unto Him! You see Ladies, down here on earth as we willingly go about our duties and activities, we may find that our husbands, our children, or even our friends or family may not notice or make mention of our wholesome accomplishments. Not so with the Lord! He both sees and rewards everything.... Proverbs 31:30 is a promise that a woman that feareth the Lord SHALL be praised! Future compliments await those who seek to develop their inner nature today. God applauds a life that is not wasted in vanity but lived out in the fear of the Lord. Our heavenly Father always respects a life of sacrifice, not self-centeredness....

2 Peter 1:17, "For he received from God the Father honour and glory, when there came such a voice to him from the excellent glory, This is my beloved Son, in whom I am well pleased."

Ecclesiastes 7:18, "It is good that thou shouldst take hold of this; yea also from this withdraw not thine hand: for he that feareth God shall come forth of them all."

Psalm 147:11, "The Lord taketh pleasure in them that fear Him...."

In closing, why not bring the Lord some pleasure today - and everyday for that matter - even for all of eternity! You can be assured that the holy women of old time who adorned themselves in the fear of the Lord are enjoying the praise of the Lord this very moment for trusting in Him and not themselves. These women of virtue have long since been concerned with that which has faded away in their lives, for there is something much greater they are infatuated with....

Zech. 9:17a, "For how great is **his** goodness, and how great is **his** beauty!"

THE CONCLUSION OF THE VIRTUOUS WOMAN

Proverbs 31:31

"Give her of the fruit of her hands; and let her own works praise her in the gates."

After studying her closely, I think you would all agree the virtuous woman was definitely a fruit-bearing tree, amen? The fruit she labored to generate is what supplied her with plenty of happiness, and this woman ate well at her own hands! She favored fruit above all else and had a desire for it always. *Spiritual* fruit, that is....

Psalm 128:2 says, "For thou shalt eat the labor of thine hands: happy shalt thou be, and it shall be well with thee."

Yes, the virtuous woman makes a happy life, not only for others, but also for herself! Joy is the natural result of a life that is ordered aright; and the measure of a virtuous woman's happiness is the fruit of her *own* hands, not someone else's! She is not in the habit of blaming her situation on her husband, her children, her pastor, her mother-in-law, another woman or man at church, her neighbor, etc. Instead, a woman of virtue takes full responsibility for her own emotions; she does not live upon the labors (or lack thereof) of other people! How happy have you been of late, dear lady? Are things *well* with you? Become a "fruit inspector" today and scrutinize your life.... Have you been producing good fruit or bad fruit? The fruit you produce is the fruit you will eat thereof! Yes, what you produce not only affects others, but also brings either life or death to your very own soul. Good fruit produces joy while that rotten fruit brings with it only misery and moaning.... If you have been feeling a little "sick" at heart, you have probably harvested some bad fruit or been trying to live off of others!

Isaiah 3:10, "Say ye to the righteous, that it shall be well with him: for they shall eat the fruit of their doings."

When you see pears lying under a tree, you know the tree is a pear tree, amen? So it is with people.... Spiritual fruit is what we, as Christians, are known by; and when you claim to be a child of God, people will inspect your life closely for evidence of it. They want to know if Christianity is real or not. When you encounter the unmistakable fruits of righteousness in a person's life, you know you have found a true Christian!

Mt. 7:20 says, "Wherefore by their fruits ye shall know them."

As you inspect your own fruit today, can you be identified as a virtuous woman by what is falling from your tree? Is your fruit similar to the nourishing, godly fruits listed in Proverbs 31, or have the worms of the world come to reside in your crop? What kind of fruit have you been cultivating with the labor of your hands? Ladies, the Lord would have us to produce *holy* fruit rather than "holey" fruit, for holey fruit is good for nothing....
Romans 6:21 & 22 says, "What fruit had ye then in those things whereof ye are now ashamed? for the end of those things is death. But now being made free from sin, and become servants to God, ye have your fruit unto holiness, and the end everlasting life."

Multitudes of God's people are in the practice of producing rotten fruit and are miserable for it! Their lives are an orchard of depression and decay, void of the growth of God's grace. This world is not benefiting one bit from their testimonies, from that which is falling from their tree. Their fruit holds no nutritional value... How can you keep your fruit from rotting as a Christian? What is the secret to a plentiful, satisfying crop? Turn to John 15:3-5, where Jesus Himself gives us the answer....

"Now ye are clean through the word which I have spoken unto you. Abide in me, and I in you. As the branch cannot bear fruit of itself, except it abide in the vine; no more can ye, except ye abide in me. I am the vine, ye are the branches. He that abideth in me, and I in him, the same bringeth forth much fruit; for without me ye can do nothing."

Ladies, abiding in Christ is the secret to a good crop, to us bearing *much* fruit in our lives. We cannot do it without Jesus, and that is the trouble with many Christians today - they are living a life *independent* of the Lord God. They are attempting to thrive and survive in this world apart from abiding in the Savior's grace. They have foolishly forsaken their Bible reading and time in prayer. Attending a good Bible believing church where *truth* is preached devoid of compromise is no longer a priority. They have forsaken the counsel and guidance of the scriptures and rejected the authority of the shepherd God has placed over them. Listen, when you cut yourself off from God, you will die! Abiding in Christ is essential to a joyful, *fruitful* life as a Christian; it does not come any other way! God's Word keeps our hearts and lives clean, and encourages the production of good fruit season after season over the course of our lifetime. As soon as you turn your back upon the Lord and His ways, your fruit begins to wither and rot and the worms of the world are able to take over the remains of your life. We then waste that which *could* bring glory to God and hope to a lost and dying world....

John 15:8, "Herein is my Father glorified, that ye bear MUCH fruit...."

The virtuous woman, though exceptionally fruitful, is a woman of humility. This means she does not go about bragging of her spiritual or physical accomplishments. Self-righteousness is not a worm in her godly character! She does not pompously report to the other women she is acquainted with that she has all her housework completed and evening meal prepared by 6 a.m. She does not assemble at the gates of the city simply to boast of how she memorized the entire book of Psalms over lunch. She does not look for opportunities to broadcast how many tracts she passed out during the week. Nor does she keep a running tally of all the souls she led to Christ in order to impress others with her spirituality. Rather, her works are known in the gates *apart* from her having to be there to advertise them!! The fruit in her life speaks for itself; she needs not utter a word for the simple reason that she has a godly reputation. A woman of virtue does not require praise or acknowledgment for the godly accomplishments that she considers her *reasonable service* as a servant of the Lord! Nor does she pout if she is overlooked, or even neglected to be called upon to teach gatherings of women about orderly, godly living. Though she has experienced victory in certain areas other women might still be struggling with, a woman of virtue is not in the habit of clucking her tongue or shaking her head in disbelief at the immaturity of another. Pride has no part in this woman's ministry! Therefore, others naturally seek her out for help, guidance, and counsel due to her spirit of humility and helpfulness. Her works are magnetic, attracting people to her. She can't help that! In a humble spirit, she encourages and instructs those who come along side of her that need suitable direction. Be careful ladies, that when you master qualities of virtue you do not spoil your fruit with pride... Let your own *works* praise you, not your own *lips*!! God set it up to be that way and we would do well to heed His plan! There is nothing so unattractive and annoying as a braggadocios individual, amen?

Proverbs 27:2, "Let another man praise thee, and not thine own mouth; a stranger, <u>and not thine own lips</u>."

By the way, the word "works" in our main text is plural; did you happen to notice that? Yes, the virtuous woman is an expert and thorough juggler of *many* works - not just one. She doesn't just make the bed and then call it quits for the day! She does *all* she can; she *excels*, amen? Because of her strong work ethic, her works <u>praise</u> her; they do not bring shame to her name - or to her Savior's name! When it comes to the business of serving others and doing right in general, the virtuous woman does not have a retirement date in mind; it is her life's *work*....

She is a helper at heart (Gal. 6:2)

Christ is her example in work. (Mt. 20:28)
Her work is performed in humility. (Mk. 10:44)
Her work is wrought in cooperation with God. (1 Cor. 3:9)
Her work is coupled with willingness. (Is.1:19, 1 Tim. 6:18)
Her work is carried out with joy. (Ps. 40:8)
Her work is a prompt response to a call of duty and carried out to completion. (Jn. 17:4)
Her work is according to her ability. (1 Peter 4:11, Mk. 14:8)
Her work furnishes a pattern for imitation. (Titus 2:7)
She works well with others. (Jn. 4:36)
Her work is a result of her salvation, not for salvation. (Gal. 2:16, Ephes. 2:8 & 9)
She claims God's promises in her work. (Rom. 2:8, Mk. 9:41)
Her work is abundant. (1 Cor. 15:58)

Rev. 3:8 says, "<u>I know thy works</u>: behold I have set before thee an open door, and no man can shut it: for thou hast a little strength, and hast kept my word, and hast not denied my name."

Scripture teaches that doors are open and shut by God; He is the authority over all. As a result, the virtuous woman is presented with many opportunities at the hand of the Lord because He knows her works! She has a history of faithfulness... For this reason, the Lord can trust a woman of virtue to respond properly to His authority in her life and do the right and good thing every time to every person that crosses her path. She keeps His Word and willingly steps through the doors of service, only to find happiness waiting on the other side! Her life is proof to others that God is a God of love, strength, honor, humility, righteousness, truth, peace, power, and purity.... The virtuous woman is a testimony to God's name and her life glorifies Him.

James 2:17 says, "Even so faith, if it hath not works, is dead, being alone."

Yes, her faith was alive, for her God was alive! Because of that, the virtuous woman's works are not alone. They are mixed with faith in God! What a difference is made when we can carry out our responsibilities and duties in faith... With the Lord, there is the realization that none of our work is in vain! The faith of the Proverbs 31 woman resulted in *living* works - they never died out but kept on going. What has your faith in God done for your works, dear lady?? Has it kept them alive, or have they long since diminished...

1 Thess. 1:3, "Remembering without ceasing your work of faith, and labour of love, and patience of hope in our Lord Jesus Christ, in the sight of God and our Father."

In conclusion, will you be remembered as a virtuous woman when your life reaches its final chapter? Will your faith in God carry you to the finish line? Will your works - the fruit of your labor - praise you AND bring glory and honor to the Lord Jesus Christ, proving that His way is right and His Word is true? **"Who can find a *virtuous* woman..."?** Ladies, let us make it possible to meet one even now in this century! May the world find one in YOU!

The Rest Is Up To You

Made in the USA
San Bernardino, CA
20 June 2016